D0849023

Army of Entrepreneurs

Army of Entrepreneurs

Create an Engaged and Empowered Workforce
for Exceptional Business Growth

Foreword by Darren Hardy, *SUCCESS* magazine

Jennifer Prosek

AMACOM

American Management Association
New York • Atlanta • Brussels • Chicago • Mexico City • San Francisco
Shanghai • Tokyo • Toronto • Washington, D.C.

Bulk discounts available. For details visit:
www.amacombooks.org/go/specialsales
Or contact special sales:
Phone: 800-250-5308
E-mail: specialsls@amanet.org
View all the AMACOM titles at: www.amacombooks.org

This publication is designed to provide accurate and authoritative information in regard to the subject matter covered. It is sold with the understanding that the publisher is not engaged in rendering legal, accounting, or other professional service. If legal advice or other expert assistance is required, the services of a competent professional person should be sought.

"Army of Entrepreneurs" and "Commission for Life" are trademarks of CJP Communications.

Library of Congress Cataloging-in-Publication Data

Prosek, Jennifer.
    Army of entrepreneurs : create an engaged and empowered workforce for exceptional business growth / Jennifer Prosek.
        p.   cm.
    Includes index.
    ISBN-13: 978-0-8144-1673-0 (hardcover)
    ISBN-10: 0-8144-1673-X (hardcover)
    1. Employee motivation.   2. Management.   3. Open-book management.
4. Organizational effectiveness.   I. Title.
    HF5549.5.M63P76   2011
    658.3'14—dc22
                                                                                2010020482

About AMA

American Management Association (www.amanet.org) is a world leader in talent development, advancing the skills of individuals to drive business success. Our mission is to support the goals of individuals and organizations through a complete range of products and services, including classroom and virtual seminars, webcasts, webinars, podcasts, conferences, corporate and government solutions, business books, and research. AMA's approach to improving performance combines experiential learning—learning through doing—with opportunities for ongoing professional growth at every step of one's career journey.

Printing number

10   9   8   7   6   5   4   3   2   1

Contents

Chapter 7 **Using Technology** 98

Chapter 8 **Measuring Success** 113

Chapter 9 **Officer Training** 130

Chapter 10 **Maintaining Momentum** 144

Foreword

WE ARE LIVING IN THE AGE OF ENTREPRENEURIALISM.

Every so often the capital market reshuffles the deck. Recently the financial crisis and economic downturn disrupted the status quo and left us in a squall of unprecedented change. While in sunny times it can be difficult for entrepreneurs to punch their way into an existing market, the playing field has now been leveled and everything is up for grabs. The new kings of the economic kingdom will be crowned over the next couple of years. You could be one of them.

I am here to tell you one way to make that happen. In your hands, you are holding the vision of one entrepreneur—and what she realized she could do not just for her business, but for other businesses as well. *Army of Entrepreneurs* takes what I've long said about the benefits of entrepreneurialism and expands them into a management philosophy for the new millennium.

Here, you will learn how entrepreneur Jennifer Prosek cut through the mumbo jumbo of management theory and laid out the blueprint for her success today. You'll see how she learned to embrace entrepreneurialism and achieve her own success—and then developed that success into a system that not only built her company, but also empowered the individuals within it. You'll see how she amassed and trained her Army of Entrepreneurs. At the same time, she'll teach you how you can do the same for yourself and your employees.

Does this work? Yes. I know this not just because Jennifer Prosek says so, and not just because she presents her theories backed by interviews, experts, and analysis. I know because I see a lot of what passes for entrepreneurial advice today and I've developed a practiced eye for what's good and what's hot air. At *SUCCESS* magazine we write for the ambitious entrepreneur, the elevated subset of small business leaders seeking the competitive advantage in business. It is my business to constantly survey the landscape of entrepreneurialism and the many self-proclaimed experts in the space. All day, every day, I am consuming, sorting, filtering, and wading through the wave of information. I can quickly and easily pick out who is the real deal and who is just hoping to ride the tide. I can tell you that Jennifer Prosek and the ideas shared in her book can alter the trajectory of your life and your business. She is the real deal.

We live in exciting times. There has never been more opportunity or more ways for the average person, regardless of family background, social status, or even education, training, or experience, to create great fortunes than there are today. While it might look like a challenging time in the national or global economy, we are actually in the middle of the perfect storm for entrepreneurship. Whether you are going it alone or leading a team forward, now is the time to get started. Like Jennifer, step up and embrace the entrepreneurial spirit of the new age.

Darren Hardy
Publisher, *SUCCESS* magazine

Acknowledgments

THANK YOU FIRST TO THE ENTREPRENEURS OF CJP. THIS BOOK, and this company, could not have happened without you. Your talent, wit, and sheer work ethic have made it a pleasure to come to work every day. Special thanks to Mark Kollar, my partner and "work husband," who has supported me (and put up with me) every step along the way. Thank you also to my wonderful and valued clients.

Thank you to my family: my husband Patrick and daughter Scout, who provide the love and balance in my life that keeps me going; my brother James Prosek, whose successful career as an author inspired me to write a book; and my mom and dad, who, as immigrants to this country, taught me to value the American Dream.

Thank you to my friend and agent, Heidi Krupp of Krupp Kommunications, who convinced me that my message had value to others. As a publisher once said, "Heidi is a force of nature." I agree. Thank you to my editor, Bob Nirkind, and collaborating writer, Ellen Neuborne, for her help in molding my raw ideas into beautiful, readable chapters, and thank you to my friend and colleague David Wilk of Prospecta Publishing, who introduced me to Ellen. And special thanks to the great team at AMACOM, who believed in this project from the start and have worked tirelessly to make this book happen.

Army of
Entrepreneurs

Introduction

I WAS A FEW WEEKS INTO MY MATERNITY LEAVE WHEN I REALIZED IT: My company was *not* going under.

That had been my recurring nightmare leading up to the birth of my daughter, that the company I had joined when I was twenty-two and co-owned by the time I was thirty would founder if I were not there to run it—six or seven days a week, as was my habit.

But here I was, transitioning into motherhood, preparing for my new role as a working mom, and my company was not only doing fine, it was growing. Instead of stumbling, the firm was thriving.

This was not, I knew, a matter of luck, or even hard work. The spurt of success at my firm CJP Communications was the direct result of a strategy I had been percolating for years. Even before my expectant-mother panic, I had been working on a new way to configure my business, one that tapped the tremendous talent of the seventy-plus people in my company and inspired them to rise up and face the challenges of the day whether or not I was in the office to see it. I had amassed, trained, and deployed an Army of Entrepreneurs™ (AOE).

A what? I'll explain.

1

An AOE is, in short, an internal force of committed employees. It is a structure and a mindset that enables a business to grow beyond you—the business's founder, owner, or CEO. My goal has been to empower every member of my staff to use his or her own resources and initiative to help the business succeed. Each person develops an "owner's mindset" and becomes a powerful force for growth within the organization. An AOE is the concept that changed my company and my life.

I'm writing this book to tell you that story because you can do what I did. What I discovered was not just a way to run my own business, but perhaps a way to run any business. This is more than just a story of how I got through my maternity leave without losing my shirt. It's about how a business can survive challenging economic times and come out the other end as an engaged, motivated, growing company. Over ten years, I had been developing a strategy for a new kind of management model. The birth of my daughter crystallized the need for this—and also showed me that it really worked. I drew on the elements that had been the bedrock of my own personal success and that of my firm to come up with a plan. As I worked on it, I realized how far-reaching the concept of an AOE could be.

Why This Book Now?

The timing for this strategy could not be more critical. As business people, we face a tough financial landscape. The economy behaves in ways we don't always recognize. The truisms of previous generations are not holding up. Companies "too big to fail" have failed, and throughout the business world layoffs, losses, and dampened expectations have become the norm. To say the environment is challenging is an understatement.

I have been living through the same economic turbulence you have, and I can attest to the fact that my business model didn't just grow my company, it saved it. CJP would be half its current size if it were not for the new opportunities identified and secured in the depths of our recent downturn, not by one person but by the majority of our staff. It was everyone in the boat, pulling together at the oars, that has enabled the survival of my enterprise.

Even in the teeth of the recession, mine was a firm that eked out growth. Our Army is not only profitable and productive—our company has grown from one office and about $2 million in 1995 to three offices and $15 million today—its participants are happy and fulfilled by their contribution. What's more, through the worst of it, we were named among the best companies to work for in our industry by the Holmes Report's annual PR Agency Report Card.

The Army of Entrepreneurs is more than just a process for my own firm. It's one that already works in other firms and can be applied to a much wider array of corporate situations. If you are looking for a growth engine, a source of innovation, and an insurance policy against downturns and unexpected dips in the economy, this is your book. If you are a manager and you want a way to make your division or department or team more engaged and productive, I can help. In these pages, I'll show you how I did it, how you can do it, and why this is the right time for you to make this move. Like many of you, I'm not just interested in surviving. I'm in the game for the big prize. You shouldn't settle for anything less either, especially when the tools for your success are already within the walls of your company. They are your people. The trick is to transform them from staff members to soldiers, from order takers to entrepreneurs.

What This Book Will Deliver

More than just education and inspiration, *Army of Entrepreneurs* is a practical guide to how to begin and implement a program that delivers tangible results quickly and consistently. Whether you are a small-business owner looking to grow your company or you are running a business unit and are looking to stimulate innovation, this book unveils a time-tested model for success.

What you'll get in these pages is:

♦ An easy-to-follow, replicable plan of action that can be instituted quickly and inexpensively

♦ Anecdotes and case studies that illustrate the AOE model in real-world situations

♦ Statistics, research, and commentary from experts in the business community

And while my first goal is to increase your revenue and profit, I also promise to increase psychic income—for you and for your entire team. Nothing, and I underscore nothing, has brought me more personal pleasure at this point in my career than identifying, nurturing, and watching the entrepreneurial spirit grow within my company—especially among those who didn't think it was possible.

Join me and prepare to march forward.

Part I

Taking a New Approach to Building Your Business

CHAPTER 1

Creating a
Commission for Life

SUPPOSE I TOLD YOU THAT THE SMALLEST PROFESSIONAL ACTION on your part could result in a lifelong payday. Suppose I told you it didn't matter what your rank in the company or the terms of your pay package or the vitality of your social network. Do this one, basic action, and you get the check. Would you try?

The answer is yes. I already know that. Because what I've just described to you is a system I call Commission for Life™, and it became the first building block of my new management model—the cornerstone of an Army of Entrepreneurs.

Not only would you try, but everyone in your company would try, from the interns to the executives. I've seen it happen. In this chapter, I'll introduce you to the Commission for Life system. I'll tell you how I came to it, how it works, and why it is the powerful motivational force that makes change and growth possible.

How the Army of Entrepreneurs Started

I can't say there was a "light bulb moment" for me in creating the AOE model. It was more like an evolution in my thinking.

I was always one to think big. As a child, I developed board games and sent them off to Parker Brothers. I made up advertising jingles, tag lines, and slogans and tried them out on the school bus. While I never sold any of my early ideas, that was okay. I was always fascinated that ideas, words, or images could change behavior and motivate people. Public relations was a natural fit for me.

When I graduated from Miami University in Ohio with a degree in English, I had my heart set on a job at a sexy, prestigious New York firm. But it was 1991 and there was a recession, and I took the only job available to me. I became the third employee at Stratford, Connecticut–based Jacobs & Associates, a fledgling agency that had only recently moved from the basement of Dan Jacobs's house. Still, I took the job seriously, down to the very smallest details. For example, after telling Dan for weeks that we needed a cleaning service to come in so the bathroom would sparkle for clients, Dan had only said he'd look into it. Finally one Saturday morning, I donned yellow rubber gloves and took on the job myself.

In my early years at the company, this all-in strategy worked well for me. I was emerging as a natural and prolific rainmaker. I brought in a new client between my job interview and my first day, a referral from my stepfather. Shortly after, I sold a video project to an existing client, an ambulance company. Dan came into my office with $1,000 in cash as a reward. It was a lot of money and, even more important, it was terrific recognition. I felt great. I knew I had found my calling. I loved thinking creatively about a challenge. I also discovered I had a real talent for media pitching and client relations, two pillars of public relations. Perhaps most significantly, I also figured out pretty quickly that generating new business was my ticket to an almost limitless future.

By the time I was twenty-five, Dan had made me a partner. I turned down a job offer from a prestigious New York firm to put my heart and soul into growing Jacobs & Prosek. But soon that proved less than fulfilling. I persevered through five years of steady but single-digit growth and felt totally stuck. We were growing—but not at the rate I thought we could achieve. I wanted world domination, damn it! I grew increasingly frustrated with my colleagues and staff. I had come to the conclusion that there was very little motivation and natural entrepreneurial talent around me. I didn't understand why, but my coworkers just didn't seem to "get" the business. More than once I found myself wondering, "Why didn't he see that opportunity to expand the account?" or "Her dad is best friends with the CEO of Xerox. Why didn't she suggest a meeting?" We had incredible practitioners to execute the work, but comparatively few to generate that work. I felt like the responsibility of generating new business fell largely to me.

Something had to change. I tried talking with other PR firm owners and small-business entrepreneurs. I sought out CEOs in a range of professional services businesses. What I found was lots of understanding and sympathy but few practical solutions. That's when I began to realize two things:

1. My crisis was not unique.
2. My crisis threatened everyone at the company, not just me.

I recognized that I was close to burnout, and I began to learn how prevalent and dangerous this situation was to companies. The business world is full of studies showing how entrepreneurial burnout can kill a good company. In the early 1990s, Case Western Reserve professor Richard L. Osborne studied twenty-six entrepreneurial firms and found that overwhelmed owner-managers often lead to stalled growth. In the early years, Osborne noted, these individuals invest Herculean amounts of time and effort into making the business a success. But that level of energy is tough to sustain. When the owner-manager finds himself or herself frustrated by the eighteen-hour days, the exposure to risk, the absence of family time, and the single-minded lifestyle, he or she may falter: "[W]hen the entrepreneur's vision dims and the impulse to achieve diminishes, the company frequently experiences a rapid, sometimes tragic, power failure."[1]

I recognized I could not allow this sort of power failure to happen at CJP, not after all I had invested, working six and seven days a week and even scrubbing the toilets to make it a success. And yet it was clear that I could not go on the way I was going—feeling like I was the only one responsible for generating the company's growth.

Like many other entrepreneurs, I had reached an impasse. I needed help to grow the business. This is a point at which many other entrepreneurs make major changes in the way they do business: they sell a stake, or take on new partners, or involve themselves in new joint ventures. I had a different idea. I decided I would create a new culture in my company, one that would essentially clone me. I needed a firm made up of rainmakers, innovators, creative thinkers, and smart businesspeople. I needed an internal Army of Entrepreneurs.

Amassing the Army

I took a fresh look at my own staff. At this juncture—the mid-1990s—I had bought out my partner and was now looking for ways to make this business prosper. As I mentioned, I was frequently frustrated with what I perceived to be a lack of initiative. Then I took a step backward. More than once people had said, "How do you bring in all that business? I could never do that."

What I realized was that even though I was a natural entrepreneur and it came easily to me, perhaps other people at the firm simply didn't have the tools, context, skills, and outlook they needed to sell the business and its capabilities. That emerged as the chief problem—and the crux of the Army strategy. It was one of those moments that change forever how you view the world. I then asked myself what in retrospect seems like an obvious question: "Jen, have you ever taught them or showed them what they need to know?" The answer, of course, was no. I had talked to my staff about the importance of generating new business and opportunity spotting, but I had never gone beyond that. I had just assumed that they understood and would take the next steps on their own. Clearly that hadn't worked. What it took was actually a change on my part to help build the staff I so desperately needed. Today, I'm a total convert. I whole-heartedly believe that everyone, no matter what their natural entre-preneurial talent, can learn and be motivated to contribute.

In addition to changing my perspective, I became a fan of what behavioral economist Richard Thaler of the University of Chicago calls the need for the "nudge." A "nudge" is a harmless bit of engi-neering that manages to attract people's attention and alter their behavior in a positive way, without actually requiring anyone to do anything at all. In other words, you unobtrusively set up the stimuli or conditions people need to act in their own best interests and for their own benefit, and they do it! A study on the creation of entrepre-neurial spirit in a corporate environment found that employees are motivated by a variety of factors, including management's willing-ness to tolerate risk, its support for innovation, and a culture of com-pany pride. But all these elements require one additional item vital to creating the kind of entrepreneurial spirit I was looking for: a financial incentive.[2]

Introducing Commission for Life

My task was to figure out how to get my staff at CJP to make better choices, ones that would benefit them as well as the company. The answer I came up with was to create opportunities for them to make more money, either by taking on new responsibilities or earning a commission. I developed what I call the Commission for Life pro-gram, where the employee who sets up a successful new business meeting—that's it, just sets up the meeting—gets 5 percent of the revenue from the account for the life of the business as long as they remain with CJP.

Why does this very simple incentive work? Because it encourages employees to align their own financial and professional goals with the company's growth and success. If they help the company grow, they see a direct and substantial benefit. And while Commission for Life was developed in a privately held small business, the construct can be applied to any company, big or small, private or public. Although awarding literal cash commission may not be possible in all situations, the idea is to create an incentive that keeps on giving across the employee's career at the company and aligns the individual's goals with the company's goals. It's the nudge you need to change the behavior.

Specifically, Commission for Life offers the following advantages for the individual and the company:

♦ It enables employees to earn money over and above base compensation, offering a competitive advantage over your competitors and a retention tool for the company.

♦ It can be done by anyone at any level since the reward goes to the employee who identified the opportunity and booked the initial meeting. Junior folks might not be able to write the proposal or do the presentation, but they can—just like their senior colleagues—identify an opportunity and book the first meeting.

♦ It reinforces teaching them the business, since the commission is paid only when the client pays the bill (that's a receivable), and there is shared celebration (and shared pain) when that business moves in and out of the company.

♦ It adds another set of eyes on the client. Even if the business generated is not managed by the person who identified it, the commission recipient has every incentive to police and support the success of that customer relationship.

♦ It spreads the task of business and idea generation across the firm, which takes the burden off the primary rainmakers. It also decentralizes power from the primary rainmakers, who in many firms are overrewarded for their contributions, and helps to spread financial gain.

- It helps identify "natural entrepreneurs" who love the hunt and can be cultivated and nurtured over time to become people who run practices within the firm.

- It is contagious, and success feeds upon itself. Believe me, once the intern brings in the largest account of the summer, everyone gets on board!

And the best part is that it's a win-win. The employee has the ability to earn money well beyond his or her base salary. At the same time, the company gets new, retained revenue generators for a relatively modest payback to the employee.

Even clients notice the difference. Here's what one client had to say about my associate, Todd:

> I don't know what goes on internally at CJP, how it motivates its employees. But with Todd, it was pretty clear from the beginning that he had a personal stake, a real sense of ownership. Frankly, I sometimes find it annoying when vendors call and then follow up. We're really busy; everything happens quickly and we get a lot of things thrown at us. But it was different with Todd. It wasn't like a scripted cold call. It was unique. He was very engaging. He seemed like a very hard worker.
>
> We've been with CJP for five years now and that hasn't changed. He wants to get the work done and do a good job. The other thing that hasn't changed is the core team, which is very unusual. Agencies usually have incredible turnover. And Todd's performance has been very consistent. After a while, agencies start to take their clients for granted. But that hasn't happened. I can see that Todd has a personal stake in the account and he's still a very hard worker. I had a good feeling about him from the beginning and it's worked out really well.

When the client says Todd "has a real sense of ownership," she is right on the money. Todd has a literal ownership in the client's business with the firm. And as the individual who made that first basic step—setting up the new business meeting—5 percent of CJP's take is his.

When you talk to Todd now, even after he's quintupled his salary and has an equity interest in the business, you get the sense that he's still marveling at his own success and how it came about.

"The opportunities I had at twenty-four, that just doesn't happen everywhere. The amount of respect I have for Jen is amazing. She inspires loyalty."

I'm touched by Todd's feelings. But I also know that I did more than be a supportive boss to inspire his loyalty. I gave him the nudge. As a result, we all won.

The Commission for Life program and the overall Army strategy isn't just about bringing in more money. (Really.) While I may have had new business generation at the top of my mind when I developed it, over the years I've come to realize that it does so much more for the health and well-being of the company as a whole. The Commission for Life incentive and the Army philosophy have spread beyond the new business arena. The concept has inspired product ideas, process improvement, and innovation generally across the firm. Once people were invited into the Army, they began to deliver on many, many fronts in a quest to be a part of the organization and make their mark. So while this strategy is certainly about bringing in revenue, it doesn't stop there. Once you deploy the Army, they march. Once people enter the Army, their confidence skyrockets and their interest in repeating the entrepreneurial behavior is piqued. Now they are part of the club, and the probability of another success is high. Once employees find their entrepreneurial sea legs, they begin contributing on a variety of levels that go beyond pure revenue generation.

Here's an example: Steve was a young professional with about five years of experience. When Steve was just an intern at our firm he secured a meeting with a financial services megafirm that is now a client thanks to his effort. With a major success under his belt, Steve's confidence skyrocketed. So what did he do? Steve, at the age of twenty-five, created a recruiting program for our firm that is now responsible for successfully identifying the majority of our entry-level hires. Thanks to his newfound understanding of the needs of the business,

Steve went out of his way—without being asked—to tackle one of the most important aspects of a professional services firm: finding, attracting, and retaining great people. His success in bringing in a new client inspired him to try other ways to improve the firm.

I'm not suggesting that all it takes to have a successful business is a Commission for Life plan. Far from it. There are many more elements to the creation of an Army of Entrepreneurs. But the Commission for Life is a critical step in the launch process. It is an undeniable attention getter. It is an opening move that will get everyone in the company focused on the changes you want to make. And it works.

What the Commission for Life approach has done for the business is clear. What it has done for me personally is probably worth mentioning. Five years ago I generated 67 percent of the new business. I was always worried about where the next client would come from or what would happen if we lost one or two, or more. While I still bear ultimate responsibility for the success of the business, I am no longer an Army of One. In 2008-2009, I brought in just 29 percent of the new business—the CJP staff brought in the rest. I am standing side by side with my comrades, my Army of Entrepreneurs.

What's Next for You?

Are you ready to make the changes that will usher in the era of Army in your own firm? Ask yourself:

♦ **Are you stuck?** For many entrepreneurial companies, there is a glorious period of early growth and then a plateau, a point at which growth becomes elusive. As the leader, you may find yourself working harder and harder—and achieving less and less. I certainly experienced that state of stuck. Although we were managing to produce growth, I felt like I was carving it out of the rock each and every day. I was frustrated and stressed and wondering why I seemed to be the only one around the place who was bringing in new business. If this sounds like you, you're ready. You're ready to stop making it all about you and bring your staff in on both the responsibilities and the glories of entrepreneurialism.

♦ **Do you have big goals?** Have you always envisioned yourself at the top of your profession and your company at the top of its industry? Are you the type who was always unwilling to settle, no matter what the contest?

♦ **Are you ready to try something new?** The AOE model is not commonplace. I use it. I've seen variations on the theme in other firms. But you won't find it everywhere. To try it requires a leap. It asks you to be willing to think of your company, your employees, and your own job in new and different ways. Are you the kind of leader willing to try a system before it's been analyzed to death?

Yes? Read on. The Army of Entrepreneurs starts with a Commission for Life. But there's much more.

SIX STEPS FORWARD:

What to Do Right After You've Read This Chapter

The first step toward creating a successful AOE is the creation of a battle plan.

1. Make a list of your goals for the company—this year, two years out, five years out. Where do you want the company to be?

2. List the accomplishments that will need to happen to make those goals a reality. More new business? Expansion of current contracts? Expansion into new markets? Product innovation?

3. List the activities that need to be taking place in the company for those goals to become a reality. More advertising? More projects in the pipeline? More meetings with potential customers?

4. List the skills each member of the firm needs to contribute to achieving the company goals. Cold calling? Project management? Networking?

5. Set a timetable for the rollout of the Army system. This is particularly important if you are going to launch a Commission for Life program. It's critical to let everyone know a start date so there will be no misunderstandings as to what business qualifies for a commission. The last thing you want is to launch your Army amid confusion over compensation. So pick a launch date. It can be the start of the new year, a new fiscal year, a new quarter, a new moon. Whatever suits you. But don't let this date be fuzzy.

6. Do your own personal soul searching. The launching of an AOE system is not all about changes in the staff. It is also about changes in you, the company leader. Are you ready to trust your staff? Are you ready to let go of some of your power so that others can take it and move forward with it? Many AOE efforts fail because the leader is not mentally committed to the process. An AOE system is different from what you've likely been experiencing. You have to ask yourself: Am I ready to change so that I can lead my staff to change so that the outlook for this company can change? It has to begin with you. If you hedge and try to insist on entrepreneurial behavior while still micromanaging the process, your process is doomed. This will never work for you. So begin by looking inward: List five things you will need to do differently in order to make an Army of Entrepreneurs a reality in your own company.

Notes

1. Richard L. Osborne, "Entrepreneurial Renewal—Preventing Professional Burnout," *Business Horizons,* November–December 1992.
2. Matthew R. Marvel, Abbie Griffin, John Hebda, and Bruce Vojak, "Examining the Technical Corporate Entrepreneurs' Motivation: Voices from the Field," *Entrepreneurship: Theory and Practice,* September 2007.

CHAPTER 2

Creating a Core Culture

CORPORATE CULTURE IS LIKE THE FOUNDATION OF A HOUSE. A
strong foundation leads to a strong house. A weak foundation por-
tends that even the best, most expensive construction will eventually
crumble. This analogy is perfectly suited to the business world. Good
companies—businesses that are thriving and filled with happy, productive workers—often cite their corporate cultures as a key compo-
nent of success.

Malcolm Gladwell, author of many illuminating essays on the
nature of business behavior in his books *The Tipping Point, Blink, Outliers,* and *What the Dog Saw,* goes so far as to stress corporate culture as
a key ingredient to overall success. It's not, he argues, a matter of
hiring the right talent or stars into your company. The star system is
a manifestation of what Gladwell calls the Talent Myth. "The Talent
Myth assumes that people make organizations smart," he writes.
"More often than not, it's the other way around."[1] The key, he says,
is making the system—that is, the organization itself and the way it
treats people—the star.

The questions for business leaders are clear: How do I build that system? What can I do to create the corporate culture that will build the strong house? In this chapter, I'll discuss the elements I have found to be critical steps in the creation of a strong corporate culture: authenticity, commitment to people, commitment to the business, and continuous effort. Attention to these foundation elements allows the kind of culture in which the Army of Entrepreneurs can grow and thrive.

Step One Is Authenticity

If you've spent any time in the business world, you know how it is when a directive comes down from the corner office regarding a new management policy. Oh, no. Not again. What is it this week? Total Quality? Customer Centric? Silly Hat Day? In an era in which management is a favorite topic of conversation, there are almost as many theories and subsequent guides circulating as there are diet books. As a result, workers from entry level to c-suite have become jaded.

This means that your first step, if you are to build a culture supportive of an AOE, is to demonstrate that no matter what has come before—in this job or in other jobs—you are for real. You are serious about your commitment to creating an Army-ready culture. You believe it, you are willing to live and breathe it, and you want, expect, and trust that everyone in the company will do the same. In other words, you must make the system into a star.

How do you make this authenticity pitch read, well, authentic?

Work hard at it yourself. This may sound like a given, but it's not. Managers must work as hard as everyone else. The CEO or partners must lead by example. Nothing kills a culture faster than CEOs and managers who fail to live by their own rules.

Crucial to the success of an AOE is a culture of hard work, one that extends from the top brass to the most junior employee. Entrepreneurs work hard, not only for fame or financial gain, but because they are truly passionate. This is a standard that must be practiced at all levels of the company, but most visibly at the top, for all to see.

Remember my story about coming in on Saturday to clean the bathrooms so they would sparkle for the client? When my boss, Dan, arrived unexpectedly that morning and saw me in my yellow rubber gloves, he said, "You treat this business like it's your own."

Adopt transparency and honesty in all aspects of the business. At my firm you can know *anything* about the company—short of an individual's personal compensation. Want to know my travel schedule? How many new clients we landed this year? Last year's profit margin? Whatever happened to Client X? The information is available. We take it that far. We do not keep secrets. We do not operate on the old "need to know" system.

As far as I'm concerned, we all need to know everything. That's how we can all make smart, swift decisions for the business. One of the reasons employees often hold back from making bold moves is that they're afraid; they're concerned that somehow they will trip an unseen wire and their effort will somehow be viewed negatively. This is the kind of inertia that is rampant in companies without transparency. When individual workers don't understand how the company really works, they are hesitant and careful. They want to avoid making a wrong move.

But if you know everything there is to know about how your company works, you can't make a wrong move (at least not by accident). You know as well as any executive what the company needs and what moves will bring a positive result. For years, business has used knowledge to control people. My philosophy is that control has a price. If you wield all the power, then your people can't move without your orders. If what you really want is to empower them to be entrepreneurial in their thinking and in their actions, you must give them what the entrepreneur naturally has: knowledge of what's going on in the company.

Transparency often breeds the kind of loyalty other firms envy. Ken Anderson, founder of engineering design firm Anderson Associates, based in Blacksburg, Virginia, practices open-book management, in which the financials of the firm are available via company intranet to any employee at any time: "[W]e do have a great deal of trust here, and our employees stick with us. When we have tough financial times, our 170 employees know that nobody's siphoning off money from the company and that they've got to make the pie bigger if they're going to get a bigger piece."[2]

Strive for overcommunication. An important element of transparency is ongoing communication. And when you're trying to create a culture of entrepreneurialism, you can never communicate too much. You are sharing with your team the very workings of your brain and encouraging them to do the same in return. This is the no-walls strategy of communicating, and it serves to take many different people and help them to all be on the same page, with the same purpose.

When I say I overcommunicate, I'm not exaggerating. You could even call what I do "Aggressive Communication." Every Monday I write an honest internal blog to the staff, updating them on the status of the company, the challenges facing the business that week, the state of the economic environment, and whatever else I think should be out there for discussion. Every month we have a staff meeting. Every quarter we have a professional development session. Twice a year we have company offsite gatherings.

I encourage all kinds of communication: Instant message, social media, and collaborative tools are all allowed. I am often surprised when I hear about other companies banning them. How can that be good for a company? When a new gadget comes out, I want to know who's using it and how it can help us.

Overcommunication is critical at all times, but especially in challenging ones. In difficult times, overcommunication allows the team to stay engaged, informed, and moving ahead. This is particularly important when the rumor mill can threaten productivity. I experienced this in my own company when, during the recent downturn in the economy, our business not only survived but thrived. It was thanks to consistent, open communication that we were all able to trust one another to band together and push forward through the obstacles.

Step Two Is a Commitment to People

A culture is not a static object; it's an ecosystem. It is made up of living organisms that grow and thrive—or wither and droop—based on the surrounding environment. You can't just set up a system for a culture and expect it to run because all the parts are in place. A corporate culture is an expression of the human experience inside a particular company. Therefore, the treatment, care, and training of the human beings are critical to the culture's success.

How do you show your commitment to people in your organization?

Institutionalize celebration. At CJP, we are champions and public cheerleaders for great work and the contributions of all members of the Army. Nothing is more frustrating than the prospect of working hard and having nobody notice. Except, of course, the prospect of working hard and having the boss take all the credit.

In an AOE environment, successes are noted, celebrated, and set as standards for continued excellence. We never miss a chance to tell each other that we have done a good job. We have many vehicles for celebration at our firm. Among them is our monthly staff meeting that ends with a "pat on the back" session, where colleagues thank other colleagues for moments of greatness. Whether it's a result that won kudos among clients, an instance where a colleague covered a sick day for another flawlessly, or an idea that brought revenue into the company, the pat on the back is our public display of affection and gratitude for one another.

Offer professional development. It is unreasonable to demand excellence without providing the tools necessary to achieve it. One of those tools comes in the form of training. Never make assumptions that people cannot or do not want to learn or do something. Instead, always ask yourself: Have I trained that individual to master the skills I want and need? We believe in a constant environment of teaching, training, and learning.

It is my core belief that people can learn anything and that once you stop learning you should look for another career. We start the process the day you arrive at our door. We make sure that every new person is taken out to lunch by an AOE role model and told, very specifically, how to be successful at our firm. This simple extension of informal mentorship has accelerated the success of many employees. Rather than having to figure it out, it is presented to them. We even provide a script of sorts to the mentor, to ensure that the key points are communicated and that the lunch serves both its social and training purposes.

Encourage autonomy. Old fashioned, punch-the-clock policies are a turnoff to entrepreneurs. Commit to trusting your employees to do their jobs, even when it seems they are wandering outside the lines of their job descriptions. Allowing people to stretch their wings, experiment with new technologies, and implement their own ideas is a big part of our culture.

A good example is Wilson, who led CJP's early efforts in digital and social media. While Wilson did great work for his clients, which were primarily tech and professional services companies, he also had another passion—entertainment. A former actor who played a regular character on the Boston University–produced student soap opera *Bay State*, Wilson also loved theater, movies, music, and popular culture. Just for fun, he made a CJP-centric movie for an offsite meeting. It was a takeoff on horror movies, filled with inside jokes and gentle pokes at people. It was also really funny and people loved it.

Fast forward a few years. A staffing agency client was looking for a way to break through the marketplace clutter and appeal to younger people, who typically get much of their entertainment and information online. As a way to meet the client's goals, Wilson suggested a satiric look at the unglamorous world of temporary workers called *The Temp Life*.

The client loved it and Wilson wrote, directed, performed in, and edited a scripted web series about a fictional staffing company with clueless leadership and zany clients. Now in its fourth season, *The Temp Life* was also recognized by *Brandweek* as one of the "brightest ideas" of 2008.

But that's not the end of the story. With the full backing and support of CJP, Wilson went on to form CJP Studios, which creates a range of branded shows, brokers licensing deals, and provides PR for other entertainment properties.

Would Wilson have had that opportunity somewhere else? Perhaps. But at CJP, he was given the time and resources he needed to succeed. As a result, CJP developed a new and powerful suite of client offerings and Wilson has carved out a career that brings together his knowledge, skills, and passions. The autonomy we allowed one employee not only launched a now-profitable practice for the firm, but it also helped make CJP a good home for his brilliance and creativity. Had we insisted he stick to his job description, how long would he have stuck around?

Provide challenge. Complexity is not a barrier to success—it is an inspiration to action. Making the job too rote and too mind-numbing will only produce automatons. To get the most out of your Army, challenge them beyond what they thought was possible. Push them to achieve at even higher levels next time. Encourage them to encourage each other. A colleague came to her performance review recently with a chart titled "What I'm Most Proud Of This Year." Listed on that page were eight different types of work she'd tackled in the past twelve months, all of which were in new disciplines for her.

Step Three Is a Commitment to the Business

Ultimately, it is all about the success of the company. Attention to people, attention to authenticity, all must be in service to the ultimate goal: the growth and achievement of the firm. This is why we're all here. This is what will make all our efforts worthwhile.

What can you do to make that happen?

Present financial rewards that match contributions. I discussed this in detail in Chapter 1 and the focus on Commission for Life. Individual success must be tied to company success. The more closely those two are aligned, the better. A study by HR consulting firm Watson Wyatt underscores the importance of linking pay to performance and offering that link to all employees: "For example, if the CEO has a salary, the opportunity for a bonus and stock options, so should his division managers, his salespeople and his assistant. That way, they share risk, they share opportunity, and they share reward," said Ira Kay, Ph.D., practice director, compensation for Watson Wyatt Worldwide.[3]

Insist on deal breakers and zero tolerance. We have a clear set of guidelines regarding business practices and ethics. We consider these elements our belief system and they are not applied haphazardly. When people bend and break those barriers, we let them go. No one is excused from the behavior standards we have set as a firm. This is not a process we set up to punish people. It's a way to be clear with everyone that what we say is what we believe and it is how we will act.

This is a critical stance for us, not just for moral reasons, but also for financial ones. Studies show that ethics has become an increasingly important criterion for workers. Research firm LRN found 94 percent of employees said it is either critical or important that the company they work for is ethical, and 82 percent said they would rather be paid less but work at a company that had ethical business practices.

More than one-third had left a job because they disagreed with the ethical stance and behavior of either a manager or fellow employee.[4] If you're committed to creating a system that trains and nurtures star performers, ethics must be an ongoing commitment. You can't hope to achieve success if you're allowing a corporate culture of double standards.

Step Four Is Continuous Effort

Here is the one way a corporate culture is not like the foundation of a house. When you build the foundation of a house, you do it once. Then you move on to other elements of the construction. When you are building a corporate culture, your work is ongoing. You are always looking for ways to improve communication, improve training, and provide more challenge. You are constantly evaluating the strength of the culture and what it may need next to continue to provide the right environment for your Army of Entrepreneurs. And because the business world is always changing and your workforce will change and grow as well, your culture must also be ready to change and grow. To be sure, your core elements will remain in place. But you can never say, "All done. Moving on" and walk away from the project of creating a core culture. The culture, like the business itself, is a life's work. It is a foundation, but a dynamic one that responds to your constant attention. I am constantly reminded that at CJP our culture is an ever-evolving state that inspires and moves us toward our best efforts every day.

A colleague of mine sent me an e-mail a few years back about the firm prior to an offsite meeting I was planning. I have kept that e-mail close to me since the day she sent it, because it summed up the importance of collaboration in creating an authentic culture that people believe in:

What makes CJP such an amazing place to work is the commitment we individually make to keeping the core company a living, breathing, adaptable, fun environment. Although client work is the reason we are here and our priority is to add value to our clients, the people who are seen as true stars in this firm are those people who also make themselves a value add to CJP. If someone wants to become entrenched in this environment, their first priority is stellar results for their client; secondly it's finding a way they can grow and cultivate the atmosphere around us. If everyone does their personal part to cultivate stellar client relations and grow our culture internally, CJP will continue to rise to the top!

This is the kind of feedback that reminds me what I'm doing when I spend so much time and effort thinking and writing and managing around culture issues. When I think about it, most of the things that are expressions of our culture—our blog, our recruiting program, the way we introduce folks to their first day on the job—were proposed, created, and "owned" by the folks on the front lines, not by management.

This participation and collaboration in building who we are and what we are has defined us. The people make the system, and as Gladwell advised, the system has become the star.

Conclusion: Culture Isn't Optional

For some companies it will be quite easy to create your Army of Entrepreneurs and install the necessary incentives; for others it will be a major effort. But ultimately it has to be done. The next generation of workers is already coming into the workplace with a new set of expectations and needs. The next round of your competition is already building ways to collaborate and engage and inspire the best in your industry's workforce.

Culture has never been more critical to business success than it is today. A study by Spherion shows clearly that culture is a key reason workers work hard. Workers are not satisfied with a nine-to-five relationship with their employers. They are looking for a deeper connection, one that is in tune with their personal values. They are looking, says the firm's 2009 Emerging Workforce Study, for the company to communicate a mission they can embrace: "75% of workers agree that their job means more to them than just a way to earn a living? Clarity and commitment to a company mission, it turns out, have the power to change the role of employees from spectators to active participants."[5] When that mission is in place, the result is an engaged and productive workforce. Companies can achieve that state by clarifying and communicating what the business stands for.

Case Study: Edward Jones

One of my favorite companies to watch for corporate culture success is the brokerage and investment advisory firm Edward Jones. Based in St. Louis, Edward Jones is a phenom of a company. A private partnership with more than 10,000 offices across the country, the firm consistently ranks as JD Power's top broker-dealer in terms of customer satisfaction. Its financial advisers aren't Wall Street fixtures; instead, many of them live in the communities where they do business. If Goldman Sachs owns Wall Street, Edward Jones owns Main Street in cities and suburbs across North America.

Edward Jones has a distinct culture. Its brokers are known not just for their investment talent but for their authentic caring for customers. It's not unusual to hear a story of an Edward Jones broker helping an elderly client move to a new home or babysitting for a client family. Some might call their values old-fashioned, but the payoff is undeniable.

In 2008, when Lehman and Bear Stearns failed and Wall Street became synonymous with liars and villains, Edward Jones and the culture it had created for almost a hundred years became extremely appealing to individual investors looking for trustworthy advice from someone who knows them personally. Edward Jones's clients define this mindset.

Edward Jones, a private partnership, has always had an Army of Entrepreneurs. The company does not hire top MBAs or "stars" from other banks; it hires smart, eager folks and trains them. At Jones, the system is the star.

We have already seen assets flowing from large Wall Street private banks to smaller, independent brokers. Edward Jones will and should benefit; it is authentic, collaborative, communicative, and ethical. At the same time, the company is incredibly entrepreneurial and aggressive. Surely Edward Jones has stars, but in actuality it is the system that is the star, and the company's culture that has allowed it such continued success.

SIX STEPS FORWARD:

What to Do Right After You've Read This Chapter

The first step toward creating a perfect culture is to understand the one you have. Conduct a culture audit.

1. List five words or phrases that come to mind when you think of your corporate culture.
2. List five attributes of the ideal corporate culture—the one you would like to see at your firm.
3. In an anonymous survey, ask everyone on the staff to do the same. Tell them not to overthink it or discuss it amongst themselves, just list the top five things that come to mind when envisioning the current state of the corporate culture.
4. Compare the lists. Are you far apart? Do you agree on key culture attributes? Does the culture look the same to you as it does to your staff?
5. What changes need to be made so that an AOE culture can be made into a reality? List three things that can be altered, tweaked, or completely revamped to produce a desired culture element in your firm.
6. Don't try to do this in a vacuum. The creation of corporate culture is not a new phenomenon. Look around; ask your staff to do the same: What companies do you admire for their corporate culture? Ask your staff to research and report back on great corporate cultures in your industry. Have them list what they admire about the culture, what steps the company takes to make that culture a reality, and what steps might be possible within your own firm to achieve similar results.

Notes

1. Malcolm Gladwell, "The Talent Myth," *The New Yorker,* July 22, 2002.
2. Ken Anderson, "By the (Open) Book," Inc.com, September 15, 1999.

3. Ira Kay, Ph.D, and Bruce Pfau, Ph.D, *The Human Capital Edge: 21 People Management Practices Your Company Must Implement (or Avoid) to Maximize Shareholder Value* (McGraw-Hill, 2002).

4. "Ethics Impact on Employee Engagement," LRN ethics study, 2006.

5. Emerging Workforce Study, Spherion, 2009.

CHAPTER 3

Thinking Entrepreneurially—Even If You're a Big Company

I ONCE SHARED A PANEL DAIS WITH ONE OF THE MOVERS AND shakers of the Internet economy. He was the genius behind one of the most successful web-based ad networks and had founded and launched half a dozen different Internet ventures. But he wasn't always a lone ranger and he reached back into his history to tell us a story, a classic mistake big companies make when they encounter a new idea.

It was back before his ad network days, when he was a senior vice president at an established old media company that was big and growing bigger. Our speaker was excited to be part of the colossus and was instrumental in a restructuring effort that helped increase the firm's profits. But he was not the type to just sit back and follow orders. He was always thinking: How could this job be done better? What could take this company into new territory? He came up with an idea for a new line of business and proposed it to his boss. He was sure he was about to do something great for his firm.

But the answer came back: No. Not for any particular reason. Just

No. And our speaker took that as more than just a negation of his idea. He gleaned from that No that this was a company that did not and could not value his entrepreneurialism. It was just not going to work for him. So he left.

His employer made a mistake, one that is hardly unique. Many big companies would have followed the same playbook, insisting on conformity and process over entrepreneurialism and innovation. Too many companies think that constant creativity is simply better suited to smaller firms. They think there's no way an AOE system could work in their organization.

A special report by *The Economist* addressed this view as one of the five great misconceptions surrounding entrepreneurship. It is a myth, the article said, that entrepreneurship cannot flourish in big companies. It can and does. For many big firms, this support for entrepreneurial thinking is the very element that helps them compete and succeed against other giants.[1]

There was a time when business moved at a slower pace and a large firm could afford to be steady and methodical. It was prudent, then, to be careful and thoughtful and to stick with what works. The impetus for change was left to smaller, hungrier companies. But today's business world is vastly changed. Thanks to technological innovations and lightning-fast communications, the business cycle has shrunk and the speed at which companies must move has revved into higher gear. Embracing what has worked in the past is a recipe for obsolescence. Companies today must live on the constant edge of innovation or find themselves trampled by the competition and abandoned by their customers.

In this chapter, I'll argue that not only can a big company embrace entrepreneurial thinking, in today's economy it must. This is an economy that demands an AOE system, and even big companies can do it.

Why Big Companies Need Entrepreneurs

There are several important reasons to foster entrepreneurial thinking in your ranks, reasons that explain why an AOE system is valuable to a big company as well as to a small one.

To support innovation. A company that does not constantly innovate is dying. A classic example is the General Motors Corporation. GM was once synonymous with the American Dream. It embodied all the things America was proud of: manufacturing prowess, a popular and reliable product, a fair and loyal employer. But it also came to symbolize something else: a company that could not change. If there were good ideas popping around in the ranks of that company—and I suspect there were many—the firm was too hamstrung by its old processes and policies to turn them loose and let them soar. Without a way to foster and nurture innovation from within, GM underwent a painful, public decline. It was hard to watch. But it was even harder to accept the fact that it didn't have to happen. There's nothing wrong with the business the company is in; we still buy and drive cars. The problem is that GM could not embrace innovation to keep its products in line with changing consumer tastes and the changing economy. As a result, it became an anachronism. If you are a big firm today, you do not want to be like General Motors.

To keep in touch with your customers. When did GM start to slide? Many business historians trace the decline to when the company began to lose touch with its customers. Throughout the country, tastes were changing. Brands like Toyota were moving into the consumer consciousness. Issues of affordability, reliability, and energy efficiency began to loom large for buyers. But many analysts say GM didn't appear to notice. It just kept pumping out more big, gas-guzzling roadsters that had long been its mainstay. It was as if the company was blind to changes in the marketplace. An Army of Entrepreneurs does more than just generate good ideas. It becomes the eyes and ears of the company out in the marketplace. In a firm that is old-fashioned and top down, employees may not speak up when they see their employer veering off track. In an AOE environment, they are encouraged to speak up. What do you see out there in the marketplace? In what areas are we as a company succeeding? In what areas are we losing to competitors or to changing client/consumers tastes? Your Army is your connection to what's going on outside your office. Years ago, focus groups and market research would have been paid to provide feedback. Today, you need information faster and from a wider variety of sources. Empowering your employees to do this work is not just smart, it's crucial.

To retain top employees. Successful employees are always thinking. They are rarely satisfied to come in and punch a clock and just follow orders. Often they are the individuals who are coming up with new ideas, new ways to improve the business. Any manager should care deeply about keeping these top performers since they may be crucial and valuable rainmakers. One way to do that is to nurture and reward the innovative, entrepreneurial spirit many top performers share. When a smart, innovative person is told to stay within the lines and not try anything new or challenging, that individual may wonder if he or she is valued. The story I related at the opening of this chapter is a perfect example of what happens when an innovator is not supported. A wildly successful new media innovator was ready, willing, and able to try out a new idea for his employer, but he wasn't supported. Instead of simply shrugging his shoulders and returning to his cubicle, he went out and found a company that valued his entrepreneurial spirit. In that new environment, he was able to find support for his ideas and launch them successfully.

To be faster. The world moves faster and business must keep pace. An Army of Entrepreneurs is a key way a company moves quickly. It puts more minds to work on the process of innovation. It engages more brain cells in information gathering and trend spotting. Because the cornerstone of the concept is empowering your staff to take action, it cuts down on the time it takes for an idea to become a reality. If you get your ideas only from your dedicated R&D department, if it takes six months for an idea to be considered and vetted, you are moving at a distinctly twentieth-century pace. Too slow.

To be global. No business today can be hemmed in by physical location. We must all be able to do business around the world. The global economy is the reality for all of us, whatever our industry or specialty.

If you want to do business globally, you must be willing to relinquish the old command-and-control style of business. A global business happens in a variety of cultures, across a variety of time zones. Your employees must be empowered to act. If one of your vice presidents has a line on a new business venture in Hong Kong, should he have to wait until the office is open in New York to move it forward? If a staffer in New York needs to tap a resource in China to make a current client happy, should that be slowed down by a company that only understands how to do business in the United States? Calling upon your employees to take responsibility for making their jobs work is part of the AOE system. They need to look outward and adapt. Certainly that is what makes for success in the global marketplace.

Strategies for Big Companies

Many managers of big firms realize the value of entrepreneurial thinking. What's missing, from their perspective, is a way to create that mentality within the walls of a large operation. For many of these companies—especially those that have long histories and complex processes—the idea of instituting entrepreneurial thinking just seems impossible. How could that possibly work in a company of size? How can change like that come to a firm with decades of doing things a certain way? It seems daunting. For many, the thought of turning employees loose to follow their instincts rather than controlling their every move is downright scary.

This next section will deliver concrete steps you can take—and also words of wisdom from those who have made it happen. These steps provide a roadmap for those looking to undertake or jumpstart the process of injecting entrepreneurial behavior into an existing large firm. Of course, it's easier to be entrepreneurial when the company is just a handful of individuals powered up by startup funds and a dream. But an existing company can integrate the process too.

Hire right. No matter the size of the company, the Army of Entrepreneurs starts with hiring the right individuals for the demands of Army life. The hard truth is that not everyone can handle the independence. When you work in a firm like mine, you can't be the sort of individual who comes to work every day, punches a clock, does no more and no less than what you've been told, and leaves at quitting time. That kind of drone behavior won't work for me, and if you are a big firm hoping to foster entrepreneurial thinking in your staff it can't work for you either. Just as a small company looks for a self-starter, someone who is always thinking, always looking for opportunity—that's what a big firm must look for as well.

For big companies, this means instituting a key set of guidelines into the HR process. In a small company, the CEO can meet every potential new hire and determine whether the individual has what it takes to be entrepreneurial. In a big firm, that's not possible, so a process must exist to help that sorting happen.

Jim Walker, cofounder of Octagon Research Solutions, faced this issue when his firm began its growth spurt. The company went from a handful of employees to two hundred in just five years. But Walker worried constantly that the growth rate would dampen the entrepreneurial spirit he knew to be the cornerstone of its success. "We want to be a big company," he once told a reporter. "We just don't want to have a big company mentality."[2]

To combat this, Walker focused on refining the company's hiring practices:

◆ Octagon conducts team interviews so that one or two people aren't fooled by a fast-talking candidate with less-than-stellar entrepreneurial skills.

◆ The company uses a lot of behavioral questions in an interview, encouraging the candidate to reveal how he or she would react in certain situations.

◆ Its interviewers watch for "high-maintenance" people. An individual who needs a lot of hand holding and doesn't step up and do what needs doing is someone who will not thrive in an entrepreneurial environment. Nor will that individual be a strong contributor. These are the people, Walker says, who say they are entrepreneurial in the job interview, but after the first week on the job they are asking where their "admin" support is.[3]

Hiring people who think like entrepreneurs is the first step to having an entrepreneurial spirit become part of your corporate culture.

Create internal support systems. Once an entrepreneurial-minded person joins your organization, then what? Have you created a hospitable environment for his or her creativity? In a big company, the answer is often "no." Creative people with lots of new ideas find themselves bumping up against the command-and-control system that has been in place for ages. Consider again the story I told you at the start of this chapter about the individual with a great new idea for his big media employer. When he hit a wall, he left for a new job. A large part of fostering independent thinking in a big firm is laying the groundwork and creating a system where creative people will be happy and rewarded for their efforts.

An example of this is found in the consulting logs of McKinsey and Company. McKinsey was hired to help a European telecom company cope with both stiff competition from the marketplace and low morale within its ranks. The consulting firm found that the telecom company had an abundance of brainpower among its employees, but the workload most managers were assigned was so burdensome that it left little time or incentive for any of their creative people to explore new ideas.

This was hurting the company in a number of ways. First, it was creating a poor internal work environment. When people are miserable, they job hunt. You may be lulled into a sense of security during tough economic times, thinking employees will stay because they are happy to have a job, any job. But even if this is true, it is only a transient condition. As soon as the economy picks up (and it always does, eventually) your best talent is already prepped to bolt. Low morale creates a talent flight risk.

Second, it was creating a static business environment, which is death in the crowded and competitive telecom industry. If you are in an industry with lots of players and plenty of "churn" as customers are on a constant hunt for the next best deal or product, you can't afford to be still. You must constantly be innovating just to stay even.

The McKinsey solution was to create an internal corporate venture capital group tasked with fully exploiting the professional talent already in place in the company. The group's mission was to help the telecom's engineers advance new ideas and accelerate new technologies. McKinsey also assisted the company in identifying and developing the internal leaders necessary to manage a fast-moving group within the walls of a traditionally slow-moving giant.

By creating this internal group, the company was able to act entrepreneurially within its own walls. The new unit launched new products and was able to put the company into new areas of business. It was clear, McKinsey concluded, that entrepreneurialism can thrive in a big-company culture, if given the right systems and support.[4]

There's another bit of advice for a big firm embedded in the McKinsey example. The company doesn't come out and say so, but, reading between the lines, it's clear that this telecom company was able to embrace an entrepreneurial solution in part because it had outside assistance. The introduction of an outside consultant to the project helped foster change in a firm that was tangled up in the burdensome paperwork and processes of its own making. Hiring an outside consultant isn't the answer for every company—some can't possibly manage the expense. And certainly the responsibility for fostering change cannot all be hoisted onto the consultant's shoulders. You have to be ready to lead this change yourself. If not, what will happen to it when the consultant packs up and goes home? Nonetheless, for some companies, the injection of an outside force helps to propel a change in behavior.

Give it time, but not forever. A big company doesn't get big overnight. And the processes and systems a big company uses did not develop overnight. These things came into being over time. So it would be reasonable to assume that the injection of entrepreneurial behavior into a large firm would not be an overnight process. It is a cultural change, and as a result it may take time to achieve. Professor Olivier Basso, writing for the Institut de L'Enterprise in Paris, cautions big firms against assuming that an entrepreneurial strategy is a quick-fix solution.

"The very nature of a large company tends to oppose any interference with the established order," he says. "Entrepreneurial dynamics, standing for autonomy and generating creative disorder, therefore need time to acclimatize to a highly structured universe."[5]

In other words, expect the status quo to resist change. At first, the ideas you have and the beliefs held by your staff may be far apart, and it will take time for everyone to come together on the same thinking. But, that said, Basso cautions that a project should not be given unlimited time. A time frame for implementing new processes is critical to motivate everyone to work toward it. The changes need to be linked to short-term goals so they can be viewed as critical and "must do now" projects. Otherwise, your plans for fostering entrepreneurialism may be pushed to the back burner.

Incorporate entrepreneurial skills into your training program. While hiring new people with the desired mindset is key, it's also important not to leave your existing employees behind. Some may not be able to make the leap to the new way of thinking, but it's been my experience that staffers can and will learn to function entrepreneurially when they're trained to do so. Training is more than just asking for the behavior. It requires you as the facilitator to set up an educational system and enroll your staffers in it. If you want different behaviors, you have to be willing to provide the necessary training and education so that your employees possess the necessary skills to make that happen. Remember to teach your managers as well as your general staff. This may require additional leadership and coaching, as McKinsey provided for its telecom client.

Consider your reward system. Just as Commission for Life inspired the members of my staff to step up and behave entrepreneurially, a big firm must find its own reward solution so that managers are motivating employees instead of just telling them what to do. Compensation is an obvious way to reward workers for the behavior you desire. But it's not the only way. For instance, publicly recognizing good entrepreneurial ideas and behavior can make a significant difference in an employee's mindset. It can be scary to put yourself out there with a new idea; in a big company not used to this sort of individual behavior, the fear may be especially ingrained. Managers must step up and positively receive new ideas so that everyone will begin to process the notion of what has changed.

Spread risk. Most of the efforts I detail involve fostering innovations within the walls of the existing company. But some big companies may opt to support and benefit from innovation by crafting an outside partnership. Siemens Medical Solutions embraced this model, putting time and effort into establishing partnerships with universities, research centers, and other companies to share the risks of new business opportunities. This process allowed Siemens to expand its knowledge base, since any partnership involves an exchange of information. It also allowed the company to reduce its own financial risk in the innovation process.[6]

But perhaps the most important way a company can reward entrepreneurial behavior is to take it seriously. It is truly demoralizing to come up with a great idea and have it shot down. It is even more so when you feel as though you were never really given a fair hearing—perhaps because you are a young staffer or because you have suggested an idea for something truly new and unusual. Treating the idea process seriously is critical to fostering its creativity. Make sure that in your business there is a system in place for receiving, reviewing, and recognizing the ideas that come through the pipeline.

There's nothing worse than being ignored. At LetterLogic, a print services firm in Nashville, Tennessee, founder Sherry Stewart Deutschmann keeps the spotlight on new ideas in a variety of ways. One of them is so simple, it is often overlooked by overachieving companies, says Deutschmann, who was one of the 2009 Ernst & Young Entrepreneurial Winning Women, an annual program designed to accelerate the growth of high-potential businesses founded by women entrepreneurs. As Deutschmann said in an interview, Letter-Logic maintains a Suggestion Box:

> It's a mail box, right at the front door. Anybody during the month can drop a suggestion in for improving morale or a systems or process. Once a month we have an employee meeting—we close the plant for two hours and have lunch catered in. We go over the financials so everyone knows how much money we made the month before. Then, we read aloud all of the suggestions and give $100 to the best suggestion. Some of them are straightforward. For example, after about a month of our program encouraging employees to bike and walk to work, it was suggested that we install a shower. Three weeks later, we had a shower installed. Some ideas are much bigger and are just brilliant. One employee suggested we convert all our vehicles to hydrogen cell fuel boosters. She included with her suggestion the IRS form we'd need to fill out to get the tax break for doing that. I awarded a double bonus for that one. I don't go for all the suggestions. One time, someone asked: Can we have Friday keggers? I said "Sure, at your house. I'll be there!" But I'd say we implement about 80 percent of the suggestions. And a great one came recently from an MBA student who was interning with us. He suggested I let the employees pick the best suggestions of the month. Great suggestion. And we did it.

Communicate like an entrepreneur. Big companies often lapse into an information-hoarding mode in which news is distributed on a strict "need to know" basis, which can leave employees operating in the dark. This dampens innovation and entrepreneurial spirit. Why would anyone be willing to take a risk in such a blind environment? Big companies can work against this by communicating in the free and open way small entrepreneurial firms do as a matter of course. But to make it work, it requires a senior-level commitment to this type of open communication.

Johnson & Johnson is one company that fosters communication across its divisions—no small task since the company is made up of more than two hundred operating companies spread across three business sectors. Johnson & Johnson set up its own Internet so that its scientists could go online and see what others in the company are working on, and communicate with each other. It encourages collaboration between specialties. For example, a team from its pharmaceuticals division collaborated with a team of engineers from its medical devices division and the result was a new product that delivered medicine to patients with cardiovascular disease via a stent.[7] Encouraging employees to communicate across boundaries creates an environment in which innovation and entrepreneurial spirit are bolstered.

Case Study: The Ernst & Young Blueprint

It is not easy to maintain an innovation culture, and business leaders must keep the flame alive as the company grows, says Maria Pinelli, Americas Director of Strategic Growth Markets for Ernst & Young LLP. Pinelli shepherds the annual Ernst & Young Entrepreneur Of The Year® Awards and has seen up close what successful entrepreneurs are able to accomplish. Often, she says, keeping a company on the cutting edge rests on the ability of its leadership to stay committed to entrepreneurialism, even as the allure of corporate structure beckons.

"It is hard and there is always a tension between the need for structure and process as a business grows and the need to keep entrepreneurial thinking alive," Pinelli says. "But you can't have one without the other and be successful. You need both, and to achieve that, a company needs a leader that can bring those two themes together."

Entrepreneurial thinking is not just for small firms, she says. For companies that are already large, the goal is to rediscover the entrepreneurial spirit that built them. For that, Pinelli offers these suggestions for nurturing and maintaining innovation:

1. Accept uncertainty. Don't fall into the trap of relying solely on data-driven planning and forecasting. Consider more real-time decision making.
2. Use innovation to reshape business practices. "Innovation is not just about new products and services," she says. "It can also be about business process."
3. Deploy human capital strategically. Slow times in the business can be prime time to ask employees to focus on innovative solutions.
4. Adopt an inclusive approach to building a global workforce. A diverse work group has the advantage of a variety of backgrounds, skills, and viewpoints. This is often the best recipe for innovative thinking.[8]

SIX STEPS FORWARD:

What to Do Right After You've Read This Chapter

To create the AOE process within a large organization, you will need to marshal support for the concept.

1. Research success stories. Look for other companies in your industry that have created and benefited from an entrepreneurial culture within a large corporate framework.
2. Create a financial imperative. Nothing starts a change in a big company faster than a strong cost-benefit analysis. Begin amassing information that shows why an AOE environment would either generate new revenues or save money within the existing structure. Look for other firms that have had measurable success and studies that support your theory.
3. Bring in speakers. Large companies often have internal affinity groups. Reach out to entrepreneurial-thinking experts and bring them in as brown-bag lunch speakers or development workshop leaders.

4. Create a cross-departmental team to explore entrepreneurial issues throughout the organization.

5. Empower a section of your own division to experiment with the process. Create your own case-study scenario. Charge a group under your command with creating a mini Army of Entrepreneurs. Track the experience of the group for use as an example for future efforts.

6. Look for what's already under way. What types of entrepreneurial activities are already at work in your company? What can you do to support, highlight, and expand those efforts? Perhaps the Army does not need to be created from scratch but can be molded from an existing program.

Notes

1. "Special Report—Global Heroes, A Special Report on Entrepreneurship," *The Economist*, March 14, 2009.

2. Ray Marano, "Big Company, Small Company," *Smart Business Philadelphia*, June 2006.

3. Ibid.

4. McKinsey & Company, "Entrepreneurialism Thrives in a 'Big Company' Culture," http://www.mckinsey.com/aboutus/whatwedo/workexamples/entrepreneurialism.asp.

5. Olivier Basso and Thomas Legrain, with preface by Giles Pelisson, "Entrepreneurial Dynamics in Large Groups," Institut de L'Enterprise, December 2004.

6. "Can Large Companies Be Entrepreneurial?" Knowledge@emory, November 2003, http://knowledge.emory.edu/article.cfm?articleid=720.

7. "Johnson & Johnson CEO William Weldon: Leadership in a Decentralized Company," Knowledge@Wharton, June 2008, http://knowledge.wharton.upenn.edu/article.cfm?articleid=2003.

8. Ernst & Young, "Entrepreneurship and Innovation: The Keys to Global Economic Recovery" (2009).

Part II
Developing an Action Plan

CHAPTER 4

Teaching Your Employees the Business

In a perfect world, every new hire would arrive at the office fully trained and educated to succeed. Imagine if you had the opportunity to ensure that all your employees had the full academic grounding of a top-notch MBA. Wouldn't that save everyone a lot of headaches?

But the truth is that most employees will arrive at your doorstep in need of training. It's especially vital for a company following an AOE strategy. When you ask your people to step up and deliver, you are responsible for ensuring that they are properly trained to do the job. So if you can't rely on the academic world to provide the necessary grounding, what can you do?

The answer is a formal training program, one that not only teaches employees their job skills, but also teaches them the business. In this chapter, I'll discuss why a formal training program is crucial for the success of an Army of Entrepreneurs. I'll take you through the program I developed for my company and tell you how other firms educated their employees as to how their business operates.

Why a Formal Training Program for Your Employees?

I want to begin by addressing a common misconception among firms that embrace the entrepreneurial spirit. Many small companies—and companies that like to retain a small-firm feel—think a formal training program is, well, too formal. It's not uncommon to find an entrepreneurial firm that considers standardized training too corporate. Many are companies in which employees simply learned their craft directly from the founder. And in a very small start-up, that's not a bad way to learn. As an employee, if you can have daily contact with your boss, he or she can also act as your mentor. You can watch him or her in action and learn both directly and indirectly the ways of your job and of the business at large. This is how I learned my job.

The problem is that once the firm starts to grow, even a little bit, that informal training system starts to show strain. As the founder becomes busier, he or she cannot be as available as in the beginning. As the company grows, there are more people, and naturally not everyone can have ongoing face time with the boss. So the job of training now falls to managers, who have presumably learned from the boss and will now pass on the wisdom. Again, this sounds all well and good, but it's exactly where the training process begins to break down. In a company with no formal training process in place, the job of teaching becomes individualized. Some new employees will have a great experience, learning the wisdom of the company from a confident manager. Others will struggle when their manager is less capable of providing training. When training is uneven, you get uneven results. Some new hires will be excited, engaged, and fully motivated to succeed; others will flounder, worry about what they're doing wrong, and lose confidence in themselves.

Good training is beneficial for more than just the employee—it is a key element in the overall success of the company. Riccardo Peccei, Professor of Organisational Behaviour and Human Resource Management at King's College in London, found training to be a critical part in employee engagement—that is, the often intangible element that binds workers to their employers. Employee engagement is the emotional tie that breeds loyalty, creativity, and a desire to go above and beyond the call of duty. While studying ways to improve employee engagement, Peccei found that a systematic training and development program, combined with clear internal career paths to help staff members develop professionally and personally, resulted in benefits to both the workers and the company. The trick, he said, is the creation of clearly understood processes for education and advancement: "If employees know where they are going, they are likely to get there sooner."[1]

A study by Dale Carnegie Training also found a correlation between training and employee engagement. In the 2007 study, about two-thirds of employees said that the quality of learning and training opportunities positively influences engagement in their organizations. Companies that emphasize a "learning culture" are the ones with the most engaged workforce.[2]

An AOE is fueled by this feeling of engagement. It is the spirit of all hands pulling together that makes the system work. But that engagement doesn't develop on its own. My point in this chapter is to emphasize that the engagement springs from a learning culture. It's not a miracle of the workplace; it is derived from good, solid, committed training.

I believe entrepreneurial firms need to get over their fear of formal training. Adding it to your mix does not rob your firm of its entrepreneurial spirit. Quite the opposite. But by institutionalizing training and mentoring, you ensure that the entrepreneurial spirit of the firm can be sustained even as the company grows. This was our experience, as well as at other firms I've observed among our clients and in the business world at large.

My Method: Finder, Minder, Binder, Grinder

Here's how I trained my people at CJP.

As the firm grew and I was feeling overwhelmed, I wondered why all my clearly intelligent colleagues were not stepping up and doing the work I knew they were capable of. That's when I asked myself whether we had trained these employees and explained what we want them to do to be successful at our company.

The answer was no. We hired smart people and left it up to the informal training network—daily interactions between managers and employees—to clue them in as to what they had to do to succeed. That wasn't working for me and I was sure it wasn't working that well for the rest of the firm either. Nobody likes to have to guess. It is much less stressful to be told concretely: This is the path to success.

So I created a path. The catchy phrase I use is "Finder, Minder, Binder, Grinder." Perhaps you know it. Professional services firms sometimes use this model, and they are the four elements of a successful employee at our company. Execute on all of them and you're going to soar.

What do these words mean? I'll explain them in order of beginner to advanced skills, which is how we expect new hires to embrace them.

Grinder. The key attribute of a Grinder is efficiency. The Grinder juggles many balls in the air and seeks to amaze others with his or her ability to get a job done efficiently, effectively, and profitably. Grinders know no rank. You can find them at every level of the organization. Even top brass are expected to do a great deal of grinding. For all, the message is this: Take on a healthy workload and juggle those balls.

Minder. A top-notch Minder is a skilled people person. This is the individual who is good at managing both people and projects. Minders are organized, communicate well, and tap into their Grinder skill set to be efficient and organized. A Minder is a person everyone in the company wants to work for and with. While being a Grinder may be considered an inward-focused effort, a Minder looks out to others and focuses on what needs to be done to support, guide, and inspire them to succeed.

Binder. A Binder builds on the Minder's people skills and takes people skills one step further, looking for ways to strengthen the bond of individuals to the company. Binders are particularly important in service-oriented businesses. There is always a customer or client. A Binder is a whiz at client relationships, building the trust and fluid communication that we have found makes companies want to keep their business with us. A Binder is always alert for ways this relationship can be enhanced and tended, never taking it for granted, never assuming the business is "already won." He or she knows that binding is an ongoing task. Beyond the client roster, a Binder also understands the internal function of binding and looks for ways to keep top employees happy, fulfilled, and working for the greater good of the company and its clients. Binders are the reason clients and employees stay put, happily.

Finder. Last but certainly not least is the role of the Finder. As I discussed in Chapter 1 when I described the Commission for Life strategy, a key element of an AOE is the mindset of the rainmaker. Everyone in the company, from summer intern to CEO, must consider himself or herself a Finder of business. Finders are great listeners, constantly evaluating what they hear for potential business opportunities. Finders are also trend spotters, seeing the opportunity before it's publicly acknowledged. Finders create opportunity for the firm, either by bringing in new business, expanding existing business, or generating ideas for new products and services.

　　Everyone comes to us with a natural tendency toward one of these skills. Some are naturally efficient—they're born Grinders. Others have people skills that make them quick Minders or Binders. And some can't stop seeing new opportunities—they're the natural Finders. We don't want our employees to stop at their natural borders, however. We encourage them to come to us with their existing skills, and then to work toward acquiring the rest of the skills on this list. That's how employees at CJP will be successful. That's the path upward.

We Start Off with The Lunch

In a formal training program, you need to do much more than simply let your employees know what you want from them. You need to deliver that information in a way that is both welcomed and understood. Far too many companies simply print up a handbook or, worse, slap some content on the intranet and hope their employees read it. Good luck with that. Training must be proactive and standardized for maximum efficiency. At CJP, we start with The Lunch.

In the first days of your employment at our company, you'll be invited to lunch. It won't be a surprise; everyone in the firm knows about the "Take the New Kid to Lunch" program. But it's what happens when you get there that sets this lunch apart. We use The Lunch to have a senior staffer introduce a new hire to Finder, Minder, Binder, Grinder.

Here's how it looked to Kristina, who joined us in July 2009:

> Lauren, my new manager and lunch partner, broke out the "Finder, Minder, Binder, Grinder" mantra halfway through lunch, and once again, my excitement for this job was reinforced. I loved the idea that our company recognized that everyone has different talents, each falling into a different FMBG bucket, and each being just as important as the other.
>
> It's kind of another way of looking at how we identify good teamwork here. Some of us stand out for our ability to run out and grab new business (Finders) and some of us (me) are better at things like bonding with clients and cementing those relationships (Binders), and each one is valuable and respected here.
>
> These aren't new concepts, per se, but CJP has found a way to name and define them, which I've found to be really helpful when I

need to sit down and evaluate my strengths and weaknesses so I can become a stronger PR professional.

The Lunch also provides an important tool for managers looking to get new hires off to a strong start. This is the perspective of Kristina's lunch partner, her manager, Lauren:

> It helps bring the organization portion to our "organized chaos." If you know an entrepreneur, then you know that they spend a lot of time running around, talking on the phone, perfecting their business, meeting with clients, pulling together proposals, and networking. Imagine a whole office full of mini-entrepreneurs. Walking into that atmosphere as a new employee can be intimidating. The Finder, Minder, Binder, Grinder speech explains why the office acts and interacts the way it does and helps provide guidance for a new employee.

I make sure I provide the managers the tools they need to make The Lunch successful. Lauren, the manager, has access to a script for The Lunch. She's given this speech about ten times now, so it's no longer something she needs. But in the beginning, when we were first developing our training program and first asking managers to take new hires out for The Lunch, I created a presentation for them to work from. Just as I am clearly laying out for new employees what I expect from them, I am clearly laying out for managers what I expect them to achieve during The Lunch. I need them to hit these four elements and to explain them in such a way that I know the core values are being communicated to the newcomer.

When does The Lunch happen? Shortly after a new employee joins us, we want to be clear that this is a firm that values training and success and is willing to provide the tools for both. There's no wondering how to get ahead at our firm. I've already learned that leaving it up to employees to figure out is rough on them and rough on me. I take a much more structured and proactive approach now to communicating what's expected.

We Teach More Than Skills; We Teach the Business

While FMBG is a cornerstone of our training philosophy, our formal training program does not end with the skills we want our employees to learn. One of the ways companies often fail in training is by focusing solely on what they want an employee to do and not giving that employee the opportunity to understand how that skill fits into the broader success of the organization.

The truth is that smart, motivated people want to be part of something. They want to know that what they do all day contributes not just to their own success but also to the creation of something bigger. For this reason, in addition to teaching specific skills, I advocate teaching employees the business. Let them understand—as you do—why we do what we do and what our ultimate success will look like.

Teaching employees the business is a radical concept. For many decades, corporate leaders took an almost paternalistic view of businesses, telling employees just what they needed to know to complete their own narrowly defined tasks and advising them not to worry about what was going on elsewhere in the firm. There are plenty of managers today who still subscribe to that system. But that won't produce the desired results in an Army of Entrepreneurs. To get everyone to give it 100 percent and pull together, you have to let them in on the reasons why you want certain behaviors. Understanding the broader aspects of the business helps employees see the "why" in what they do every day.

This philosophy produces results for all kinds of companies. Pool Covers Inc., based in Richmond, California, has been installing pool covers for residential customers since 1984. The company made the move to open-book management in 1996. In addition to training the employees to do their jobs, owners Bill and Bonnie Pickens began to teach them all the business. Financial statements were made available so employees could take them home. Bonnie led a weekly staff meeting at which one or two items from the statement would be discussed and explained in depth. Like CJP, Pool Covers Inc. did not reveal individual salaries, but all other financials were on the table. There was some hesitation at first. Bill and Bonnie were concerned that if their twenty-six employees could see all the numbers—which weren't that good at the time because the company was struggling—they would be demoralized. But that's not what happened.

The result was that their employees began to come up with ways to improve the company. They were able to devise processes that reduced the number of visits installers had to make to clients, improving efficiency. They suggested a new layout for the warehouse and were influential in deciding which new trucks to purchase. But beyond the individual accomplishments, what happened at Pool Covers Inc. was that by opening their books, the owners created their own Army of Entrepreneurs. When educated and trained to the ways of the business operation, employees became more engaged, more interested in stepping up and finding new and better ways to be part of a great and successful company. "It's marvelous that I don't have to make every decision and be the one turning the lights off at night," Bill says.[3]

Here's another example, this time from a larger firm: Publix Super Markets. Publix employs nearly 100,000 individuals at its retail supermarkets nationwide. And senior executives have done more than teach those workers the business; they have made them co-owners. Publix is more than 50 percent employee-owned, making it the largest firm of its kind in the country. Publix staffers are intimately connected to the everyday actions of the company. They know more than just their own roles in the firm. As shareholders, they are privy to the results and the information that make up the full spectrum of the corporation's workings.

What's the result of this ownership arrangement? Consistent excellence. For fifteen years, the company has made *BusinessWeek*'s list of Customer Service Champs.[4] Moreover, the American Customer Satisfaction Index gave Publix its highest rating.[5] And *Fortune* magazine has listed it one of the 100 Best Places to Work For in America every year since the list was created in 1998.[6] By teaching its employees the business, Publix created an AOE on a vast scale.

Different entities approach teaching the business in different ways. Procter & Gamble combines classroom, web, and on-the-job training and encourages managers to train their replacements as they move up the food chain in the company. GE is famous for schooling its rising stars in the ways of Six Sigma management theory. Even the armed forces have a system, starting all recruits out with basic training whether they are destined to command a tank or configure satellite equipment or peel potatoes. In any organization, leaders must develop a training program that creates the kind of individuals who will be ready, willing, and able to serve in their Army.

What I do is the following:

Communicate. There are no secrets at our company. Anything you want to know—short of a specific employee's salary—you can know. I do not silo off information and keep some employees in the loop and others in the dark. The old need-to-know information hierarchy is one that companies have practiced for ages but that I find outmoded today. You can't simply give employees their marching orders and expect them to work in a vacuum. In the world we live in today, powered by the Internet and the always-on state of communication, information travels. You have to be part of that ongoing conversation or your employees will feel you are disconnected from global trends.

I communicate constantly, by weekly blog, by phone and e-mail, in meetings, and in formal conversations. I do not hide what is happening in the business. If anything, I overshare. Everyone knows when we are close to landing a new client. Everyone knows when one team somewhere in the company is facing a big deadline. Everyone knows when one of us has a big success and deserves a pat on the back. The business is not a siloed structure but an open forum for communication. We all function on this plane of ongoing discussion, and as a result no one ever wonders if what he or she is doing day in and day out is valuable. In my firm, we tell each other all the time. This is not just a management process, it is a training process. In our constant flow of communication, staffers are constantly learning about what the company faces, what their colleagues do all day, and what we are all moving toward in terms of corporate goals.

Empower. You don't need six layers of corporate approval to try something at CJP. I do my best to make sure that I communicate to my employees that I trust them to do what's right for the company. Again, this is a management philosophy, but also a training philosophy, in a subtle way. When you empower people to make decisions and take responsibility for their actions, you inspire an important process; you encourage them to educate themselves. Workers who know they will be rewarded for proactive behavior don't sit around and wait for orders. They step up. And if they find they are short on information or on a necessary skill, they seek it out. In this way, empowerment is a critical training system. It turns the process back around to employees and encourages them to pursue knowledge, pursue skills, and avoid waiting passively to be spoon-fed. Go back a minute to Kristina's evaluation of her lunch. She quickly recognized her natural abilities in the Minder bucket. What is she going to do about the other three? We are communicating to her that these are the elements of success at our firm and that we trust her to do the best she can for this company. As a result, she will step up to these other three herself, looking for ways to improve her execution of what we've already told her will bring success to her and to the firm. Empowerment gives the employee the support to self-teach.

Our Ongoing Commitment to Training

No training program can be successful if it exists as a one-time or even as a once-in-a-while effort. Training must be an integral part of a company's existence. This is especially true for a company that embraces an AOE approach. As you continually ask your team to step up, take responsibility, and take risks, you must be willing to support those efforts with ongoing training and support. The business world never stops evolving, and so the learning of new skills can never stop either.

At our company, we follow initial training with mentoring. Veterans like Lauren see it as part of the ongoing system:

> I have a mentor, whom I meet with once a quarter to discuss my career path, goals, workload, etc. These meetings are about me, not clients, and they help to hone in on improving my weaknesses and exposing my strengths.

Those newer to the company find training and mentoring surrounds them as they adapt and find their way in the new firm. Kristina says:

> We have a serious open-door policy here, so it's easy to seek out advice/opinions/help from upper-level management. I also have an official mentor, whom I meet with quarterly (though in reality we have unofficial meetings a few times a week) and discuss how I'm feeling about my career path, how she thinks I can negotiate that career path, and generally offer support and opinions about my progress here.
>
> I'm someone who loves consistent feedback, so this is something that really helps drive me forward. On the group level, we also have professional development offsite meetings on a quarterly basis. We're not a huge agency, and I've spent my career at smaller agencies, and will say this is such a rare opportunity. Since joining, I've been to three professional development days, and each one was amazing.

What Kristina is experiencing is the second level of training, the stage at which formal training is met and supported by informal learning. The fact that she feels she can walk through an open door and talk to an upper-level manager is not just a nice aspect of her workplace; it's a critical element of how employees are trained.

Even companies with great formal learning programs can forget to support the informal learning, and that's often a huge gap that undermines the education of an Army. As important as structured training is, informal learning is what employees come to count on for their ongoing success. Studies show that informal learning is an important part of the financial equation of any company. A study by the American Society of Training and Development found that 46 percent of workers surveyed say that informal learning enhances the performance of both individuals and organizations.[7]

As much as I think a structured program of teaching employees both their jobs and the business is important, I can't emphasize enough the need to make informal learning a part of the corporate culture. This is critical for a trained AOE to continue to function and thrive, even after the formal education process has ended.

Ultimately, the key is commitment to training as a structured and ongoing effort. It may sound appealing to make training informal and less "corporate," but that only allows company leadership to shrug off what is really its job. Informal learning must be paired with a system of structured education. That's what creates a full-blown learning culture.

If your employees are not performing the way you want them to, stop looking at them and look in the mirror. Ask yourself whether you have trained them to perform in the way that you need. If the answer is no, the next step is clear. Create your own Finder, Minder, Binder, Grinder, a set of behaviors you know are crucial to your company's success. Make those attributes the core of your training effort.

Never assume your staff doesn't want to learn—or can't learn. Instead, assume they can, and that it's your job to bring that level of learning to your company.

Case Study: Federal Warehouse Company

One good example of a company that has thrived under open-book management is Federal Warehouse Company, based in East Peoria, Illinois. This was a firm with three hundred employees, about $35 million in sales, and a business in warehousing and logistics. In short, it moved a lot of stuff for a lot of corporate customers. What could it gain by teaching its employees the details of the business?

In the first year of open-book management, net income tripled. In the second year, profitability grew another 30 percent.

What happened? Senior executives found that when their employees understood how the business worked, they looked for ways to make it better:

♦ When they understood the cost of workers compensation, they came up with ways to improve safety and reduce claims.

♦ When they were briefed on the ways damage claims impacted profits, they devised ways to reduce claims.

The impact of open books was not automatic. Management had to do more than share the knowledge; it had to teach the employees how to process it. The company had to teach its workers how the business runs. To keep the learning culture going, all new employees underwent a week-long training program to learn the basics of the operation and the financial statements.

When employees learned the business, they began to think and act like owners. No longer was profitability some magical thing that happened behind closed doors. Instead, everyone began to understand how profitability was achieved and how each person in the company contributed to that result.

Education creates engagement. Engagement creates profitability. Companies that have trained their Armies to be skilled and knowledgeable reap the results.

SIX STEPS FORWARD:

What to Do Right After You've Read This Chapter

Like any great educator, you need to begin your teaching process with a lesson plan.

1. Do an education audit. What are you teaching already? What skills is that training process producing?

2. List the top five skills you want every employee in the company to have.

3. Research the education process. What kinds of training are going on in

your industry? Or in your marketplace? What can you learn from them? Are they providing a good example to follow? Or a cautionary tale to avoid?

4. Ask for reading recommendations. Poll your staff, your colleagues, your competitors, for great writing in your field. Often these are texts that generate the content of great training programs. Don't limit yourself to traditional book reading. Look at what's being written online, in academic journals, in consumer magazines. You're looking for great ideas that can be incorporated into your own company curriculum.

5. Tap other teachers. Certainly you are the primary force in leading your training program forward. But who else can you bring in to make that process more robust? List five people on your current staff with exceptional skills in a key area, and ask them to create workshops or brown-bag lunch sessions to share their learning with others in the company. Look outside your firm for individuals who would make great speakers or workshop leaders to tap as supplemental training partners.

6. List five things you personally need to learn to improve your own performance. Training should travel in all directions in a dynamic organization. Even leaders can learn.

Notes

1. "Employee Engagement," King's College of London/Speechly Bircham, June 2009.

2. Learning and Engagement Study, ASTD/i4cp, 2007, www.astd.org.

3. "Case Study: Pool Covers, Inc.," National Center for Employee Ownership.

4. "Customer Service Champs," *BusinessWeek*, March 5, 2007.

5. "Publix Named Top Supermarket for Customer Satisfaction," *Orlando Business Journal*, February 23, 2006.

6. "100 Best Companies to Work For in America, 2007," Great Place to Work Institute.

7. David Drickhamer, "Open Book Management: By the Numbers," *Material Handling Management*, January 1, 2006.

CHAPTER 5

Training the Troops

"THAT'S ALL VERY INTERESTING BUT I JUST DON'T KNOW HOW WE could make that work at my company."

I get that a lot.

Even after I spend time going over the many ways a company can embrace and engage an AOE spirit, people hear me and still come up with reasons why it would never work in their own businesses.

"That won't work in my industry."

"No one in my team would go for that."

"I'd get laughed out of the conference room for suggesting it."

It's not that they think the AOE method is wrong. In fact, when most people hear it they think that it's not just a great idea, it's 100 percent necessary. They just think they can't do it.

Why do people like the sound of the AOE method, but still resist it? The answer is fear. Fear of the unknown. Fear of making a mistake. Fear of taking a wrong step. In this day and age, making a mistake at a company can have huge financial consequences. This has made many managers hesitant to try anything new, even if it seems like a really good idea.

So for all of you out there who think the Army approach sounds great but don't know how you would get it going at your own company, this chapter is for you. Going forward, I'll leave much of the theoretical discussion behind and move into the concrete how-to section of the book. In the next eight chapters you'll learn how to develop, train, and manage an Army of Entrepreneurs. We're past the point of debating whether it makes sense to develop a workforce that can forge ahead, find new business, and give 110 percent every day with passion. These are the basic necessities of any business that is going to survive in today's economy. The only question now is how you can get there. In this chapter, I'll tell you how to get through the first stage of that process.

Develop a Boot Camp

All armies start out with a basic training regime, and the Army of Entrepreneurs follows that model. The first step a company must take in creating its Army is to set up a system of basic training. In the "real" army (the U.S. military) that means taking the group of recruits to a remote training camp for fifteen weeks and schooling them 24/7 in skills needed for combat. Since clearly that's not possible in the business world, the alternative is to set up a system of mandatory, scheduled, high-profile training sessions. These are not the optional brown-bag lunches a traditional HR department might host for a discussion of business topics. These are professional workshops designed to train and inspire your staff to more proactive functioning.

The four boot camp workshops are:

1. Teaching the Business
2. Hunting for New Business
3. Advanced Hunting
4. Intrapreneuring

The workshops are designed to be short and targeted. Think two hours, although that's a recommendation, not a rule. I advocate short, intense training sessions rather than the occasional day-long marathon. The goal is to get your staff thinking about these issues all the time. If there's too much time between training, it allows the impact of your teaching to wear off.

I'll explain how you can handle each one, step by step, in the rest of this chapter.

Workshop One: Teaching the Business

This workshop will be the one that most resembles a traditional classroom experience. You will be walking your group through some business basics and establishing a common vocabulary. The goal of the workshop is to get your team onto the same page of business understanding. For some, this will be review. But for many, this will be the first time they've really been asked to absorb and understand company financials. Remember that in many firms, the boss only cares if you do your job, not if you understand the larger financial workings of the firm. In your company, you are asking for a different level of participation and understanding from your troops.

Your first workshop should begin by addressing the room:

Thank you for coming, everyone. This is the first of four workshops we'll be delivering this year. They are all designed to teach you what you need to know to be successful in your own work and for the business at large. It's my goal to make sure you are fully armed to be the best you can be in your job so that we can be the best we can be in our industry.

It's my philosophy that everyone in this room is capable of great things; you wouldn't be here if I didn't believe that. But greatness doesn't happen by itself and it doesn't happen by accident. To execute on the greatness within all of us, we need the right tools and the right training. That's what you're going to get today and throughout the rest of our workshops.

These workshops will:

♦ Help you become a better entrepreneur
♦ Help you book that first new business meeting and earn your Commission for Life
♦ Help you identify project and client expansion opportunities that boost the bottom line (yours and the company's)

Today, you'll learn how our business works, how you affect the business in your day-to-day activities, and what you can do that will help both you and our business succeed.

We'll start at the very core of the concept: How does our business make money? You know what we do. But how does what all of us do every day translate into profits? That's often a mystery to many.

Focusing on the fundamentals. Why start out with the above speech? The truth is, many employees don't know how their companies make money. Most don't consider that information very important. They know their jobs, they know the parameters of their workday, but that's about all they bother to learn about the financial workings of the company that employs them. It may seem counterintuitive, especially for those of us who are hard-wired to be entrepreneurs, but many employees simply don't know or understand the fundamentals, such as how their product or service is valued in the marketplace, who their competitors are, and how the business generates profits. That's your goal for this workshop. And the rest of the session should cover the following content:

Starting at the beginning. At this stage, you'll need a concrete thumbnail description of your business and how it makes money. What follows is what I use for CJP:

Our task is deceptively simple: to get clients in front of the audience that will help them grow and prosper. To reach that goal, we employ powerful tools: creative thinking, sophisticated skills, and industry knowledge. We generate the big ideas, create the strategy, perfect the details, execute with precision, and deliver targeted, powerful results.

Create a thumbnail description for your own firm and include it in the introduction to the workshop. It is the cornerstone of what will follow.

Defining basic financial terms. Do some basic financial terms education. This discussion could justifiably come first in this workshop, but it's important to keep the engagement level of your audience in mind. If you start the day with a vocabulary lesson, you'll see eyes glaze over all over the room. I recommend beginning with the discussion of your business's core mission and then quickly moving into this next section. It's hard to teach if you are not working with a common vocabulary.

Put the following key terms up on a board or slide where everyone can see them. Put them in a paper handout as well:

- Revenue
- Expense
- Profit margin
- Receivables
- Payables
- Collections

You may have other terms that are used frequently in your own business. List them as well. Each term should have a short, clear definition and an example, preferably from your own industry. Depending upon the maturity and education level of your audience, you may want to find ways to impart this information in creative ways. For some audiences, a straightforward definition and explanation of the terms will work best. For others, a more interactive and engaging presentation, such as Business Term Jeopardy, may provide better results. Whatever you do, keep in mind that the overall goal is to get your employees comfortable with these terms. This is an important step to making them true Army members. You are training them to use the terminology of their battlefield.

One approach I've developed to help our employees grasp the concept of profitability is what I call the Back of the Envelope Formula. At CJP we tell people that if they simply consider their base salary and multiply it by three, that is the minimum revenue account load they should be carrying to be considered a profitable member of our staff. Of course it's more complicated than that, but these simple tools create "light bulb moments" that help employees understand how they fit into the bigger picture.

Here's another approach: If you've already got a Commission for Life compensation structure in place, tap the employees who are already in it to help explain the concepts. It's been my experience that once you participate in Commission for Life, the terminology becomes very clear. People receiving commissions will quickly understand the concept of receivables and collections. Because Commission for Life is paid when the client pays its invoice (versus when an invoice is issued), employees become acutely aware of how fast their clients pay. We hear the following exchange all the time as new employees enter the Commission for Life system:

"Why haven't I received my commission check this month?"

"Because the client hasn't paid. Would you like to help us with this collection?"

When you're waiting on your check, the language of that payment becomes a lot more understandable. Let employees who get it help you explain it to the rest of the room. Often, education is a process that takes multiple teachers. Don't be afraid to bring in other voices to help you make a key point.

Discussing where customers come from. Once you've completed your vocabulary lesson, you're ready to move on to another critical element of the business that few staffers understand: where customers come from. In some businesses—for instance, a grocery store—that may be perfectly clear. Customers come from the surrounding neighborhood. In a service business or a business-to-business setting, however, that can be a mystery to most workers. But the source of customers is a key driver of any business, and understanding where customers come from is the first step to being able to help attract customers.

You can begin your discussion by taking your workers through your client list and asking the following questions:

♦ Who are these clients?

♦ Where did these clients come from?

♦ How are these clients typical for our company? For our industry?

From there, move on to more advanced client topics:

♦ What makes clients stay?

♦ What makes clients go?

Examining the costs of running a business. Finally, the last part of this first workshop should focus on another area in which most employees are sorely undereducated: costs.

Not only do most employees have little understanding of the costs involved in running a business, but many of them think that the subject itself is not something they need to be worrying about. They think that costs are the headaches of accounting or HR, not something they need to bother themselves with.

In addressing the subject of costs, not only do you need to explain it, you need to show why everyone needs to understand it.

You might start by discussing the costs associated with running your business, including:

♦ Rent

♦ Insurance

♦ Marketing

♦ Salaries

I recommend keeping individual salaries confidential. Not all open-book management companies subscribe to this theory. Some argue that all financials should be out in the open. But my feeling is that while the financials of the business are everyone's business, personal salary situations should not be public knowledge. The full staff can know the overall figure devoted to salaries, and that should be enough for them to understand the impact it has on the company. What individual people earn is their own business to disclose or keep private.

By the end of the first workshop, you will have given your employees the basics of the business. They'll know how the business makes a profit, how the business attracts customers, and the key financial terms used to describe the workings of this (and really any) company.

GROUP EXERCISE. Where do clients come from? Break your audience up into groups and brainstorm where clients come from today. Where did they used to come from but now not so much? Where might they come from in the future? Have the groups talk amongst themselves and then come back and share their ideas with their colleagues.

HOMEWORK. Have each employee do his or her own "back of the envelope" calculation. Then have each one come up with three ideas that would improve his or her own personal profitability.

Workshop Two: Hunting for New Business

"Oh, I'm not any good at sales."

If I've heard that once, I've heard it dozens of times over the years from employees. Granted, I didn't hire most of them as salespeople, as opposed to those I hire in business development roles who know that sales is what's expected of them. But that's exactly the point. Every person on the team can learn to sell and make money to enrich their own bottom line and that of the company. In this workshop, you'll teach your employees the art of identifying and pursuing new business opportunities. In short, you will teach them to hunt for new business.

Once again, begin the day by addressing your room:

Now that you understand how this business works as well as your role in it, you're going to start learning the skills that will help you and help you help the company. This workshop will cover the art of hunting—that is, spotting and pursuing new business. Far too many people think hunting is a "knack" or an ability that you're either born with or not. While it's true there are some people who are clearly "born to sell," everyone else can certainly learn how to do it the old-fashioned way: by breaking down the process, understanding the rules, and practicing.

Hunting for new business is not magic. In fact, it's a very concrete and replicable process. Nothing to be scared of here!

This workshop will follow a four-part structure:

1. Demystifying the sales process
2. Developing your "opportunity-spotting" skills
3. Networking for fun and profit
4. Finding great leads right now

I am confident everyone in this room can do this. At the end of this workshop, you will be too.

Your workshop should cover the following content:

Demystifying the sales process. The biggest hurdle to hunting skills is the mental block, the "I can't do sales" mindset. Many people automatically believe that hunting or lead generation is impossible and that they will never be able to do it. Your first step is to make sales seem doable. That's at the heart of the "demystifying" section.

Your job is to assure your team that you will give them the tools and support they need. You begin by replacing their fear and apprehension with facts about new business development.

The top three things everyone needs to know about hunting:

1. It's not that time-consuming.
2. It's all about persistence.
3. The rewards are well worth the effort.

Anecdotes that make opportunity spotting seem "doable"—even fun—can go a long way toward making people feel excited and confident about their own abilities. Here's one I use:

> In our company, one of our most successful hunters sets aside forty-five minutes to an hour on Friday afternoons to research and pursue new business opportunities. Of course, he may have to follow up during the week, but much of the spade work is done in that weekly forty-five- to sixty-minute block. That's not much time, but over the past six years he has closed more than $2 million in new business and established his own financial services practice within the firm, in addition to making a very comfortable six-figure income.

Developing your opportunity-spotting skills. Often, great hunters aren't any smarter than the rest of the planet—they just listen better.

A critical step in teaching your staff how to hunt is to get them to simply turn their ears on to opportunity.

What does that mean? It means listening—in even the most mundane conversations—for the business opportunity. It means listening to the person you meet on a plane or a bus, or to the guy you see every day at the gym. Listen when you talk to them. Listen for the business opportunity.

I'm not suggesting you tell your staff to hard-sell friends and family. That's not very productive, and many of your staff won't actually do it anyway. But you do want them to have their antennae up at all times for the opening—the comment or situation that could lead to new business. Perhaps that person at the gym owns his own business and wants to grow it. Maybe the person you meet on the plane is married to the CEO of a big company you'd like to pitch. The point is not to be pushy, but to be listening, always, for the sound of new business calling. Consider any situation you're in— hanging out with friends at a barbecue—to be an opportunity to have fun, but also to meet someone who represents an opportunity.

We don't teach our employees to stalk their friends, but rather to ask the right questions that lead to opportunity. To ask what they are doing, to ask about their families (perhaps someone's spouse has the connection you'd want to pursue).

Defining the two kinds of networking. You want to begin this discussion by explaining that there are two main categories of networking: formal and informal. Formal networking is an event or gathering designed to help people make business connections. This kind of networking has evolved a lot over the past decade or so. At one time, many formal networking events involved dull speakers, uninteresting lunch companions, and bad food in an airless hotel conference room. Modern formal networking improves on that considerably. Wine tasting, sporting events, cruises and sails, cultural events—they're all networking opportunities. Make sure your staff understands that formal networking can actually be fun.

Follow that information up by emphasizing that networking can have amazing benefits. For starters, it's still the most tried-and-true method of new business development. Electronic communications and research are invaluable, but there is really no substitute for face-to-face personal interactions. Networking also offers other benefits. It is an effective way to leverage yourself and your company, and it sets the stage for continuing follow-up with a wide range of people, which leads to generating additional business leads.

Finally, encourage your staff to give as well as receive when it comes to formal networking. Perhaps someone on your staff could serve on a panel or give a talk at a networking event. That is truly one of the best ways to showcase your company's expertise and have people seek you out.

After presenting the content on formal networking, move to the next category: informal networking, where anyone from any part of your life can be a lead. I like to tell the story of how my former high school boyfriend became one of my largest clients. We dated in our sophomore year of high school, and he wound up becoming director of corporate communications of Mercedes-Benz Credit Corporation. A simple and authentic interest in catching up almost ten years ago led to one of my largest accounts.

Don't forget also that social media open up a virtually limitless range of contacts. Professionally oriented sites such as LinkedIn are particularly valuable, but don't underestimate Facebook. Who knows what your childhood friends are up to and who of their friends might be a great prospect? The point is to open your staff members' minds to the idea that anyone can turn out to be a good contact. And don't let people get away with the lame excuse that they don't have a network. Everyone has a network.

And while people in their thirties and forties and beyond may have larger networks, even entry-level people have lots of connections. In fact, one summer we had two interns who participated in our lead-generation workshop and then went out to land two of our biggest accounts. One young woman contacted the bank where she'd been an intern the prior summer. As it happened, it was looking for a new PR firm and CJP landed the account.

In the other case, our intern (now on staff) contacted a college friend who was working at a big financial services firm in Boston, and he landed a major project that ultimately turned into a long-term retainer. He is still collecting that commission three years later.

Finding great leads right now. After presenting your content, the final step in this workshop is to put it all together. Your staff is less apprehensive and maybe even excited about finding new business opportunities, and they know some key avenues to pursue. Everyone's ears are tuned to opportunity and their minds are open to possibility. So now you want to harness that energy—quickly, before they talk themselves out of it—to get some traction.

. . . .

GROUP EXERCISE. Split the team into groups of five and ask them to brainstorm low-hanging fruit opportunities. Each team then presents its best opportunities. Team members commit to making the initial contact and to a follow-up meeting—perhaps two weeks later—in which everyone will share their experiences. Typically, I have found in this exercise that there is at least one major success story, a meeting secured or a promising opportunity identified. Be sure to trumpet any hits. Success is infectious.

HOMEWORK. Have each employee research professional organizations, alumni groups, or other potential networks and then identify and attend one function in the next three months.

. . . .

Workshop Three: Advanced Hunting

The first two workshops in this collection are eye-openers for your staff. You have brought to their attention new terms, new concepts, and new opportunities to contribute to their own success as well as to the success of the company. For many, it may be the first time an employer has ever asked them to step up in that fashion, so it's important to let some time pass between the early workshops and these second-half workshops. You want to give your staff a chance to absorb and try out the new elements. Let them calculate their own profitability and begin working to improve it. Let them brainstorm new ways to find clients, maybe even create the opportunity to participate in the Commission for Life system. And be sure to celebrate these efforts so that everyone can see what's going on. Success, like everything else in the business, should be transparent.

Then it's time to move on to more advanced techniques. First up, advanced hunting. Here's the way I describe it:

The first hunting we learned is what I call "opportunistic" hunting. We've already shared with you the skills you need to be an opportunistic hunter. In short, you focus on your potential opportunities: your friends, family, neighbors, and acquaintances. Keep your ears in listening mode; keep the opportunity antenna up and active.

After opportunistic hunting has been mastered, it's time to move on to the next level. I call this "strategic" hunting, or strategic lead generation, which is more targeted. Strategic lead generation comes from analyzing the business's current footprint and determining where the natural extensions are. For example, in my business, we represent a number of energy and alternative energy companies. Given this grouping of clients and the experience we have built up in the sector, it just makes sense to prospect complementary, noncompetitive clients.

From that introduction, you'll then move into the body of the workshop, which is an outline of tactics that make up strategic hunting. Your workshop should cover the following content:

Reading the economic trends. What industries are on the rise? How might your firm capitalize on that surge?

Knowing the company's capabilities and areas of expertise. Encourage your staff to know more than just their own jobs and even the general skills housed within the firm. They need to be fully conversant in what your company does well, better than others in the industry. When they target a new client, they need to come in armed to answer any question about the company's work.

Learning about the prospect. In the Internet age, there is no excuse for failing to fully research a strategic prospect. In addition to company information, encourage staffers to look for analysts' reports, industry information, and even customer comments. Research the prospect's competition as well. Know that prospect's business inside and out.

Being able to answer the "why now?" question. Any prospect may rightly ask why this is a good time to do business with your firm. Can your staffers answer that convincingly? Encourage them to practice this conversation before taking on a meeting.

Knowing what services/expertise/ideas might be most appealing. Teach your staff to avoid the dreaded "info dump" in which they just shovel out every item of information they can think of in the hopes that something will stick. That's not something that will make a prospect think highly of your company. Prospects don't really want to know about the company; they want to know what the company can do for them. What your company does for anyone else is not really their concern. Encourage staffers to identify which products or services would be best suited to a prospect.

Preparing case studies and examples. Prepare background on clients that will impress your prospect. It's not about how glowing the endorsement is; it's about how impressed the prospect will be when reading it.

Planning for the first meeting—and beyond. Encourage preparation for more than just the first meeting. Map out the full courtship. Be researched and prepared for each step of the process.

. . . .

GROUP EXERCISE. Have people gather in groups of four or five. Each group discusses its best opportunistic or strategic leads, then decides which ones have the most potential. Each group writes down its pitches and elects one or two people to execute the call to the prospect and secure the meeting. The whole team discusses how to make the outreach as compelling as possible.

HOMEWORK. Each staffer should generate a list of three potential strategic targets.

. . . .

Workshop Four: Intrapreneuring

I save this workshop for last because I want the staff to think about reaching outside to new clients and new business before they turn their efforts back inward. It's not unusual for employees to be afraid to reach outside the confines of the company for new business, new profitability. So I would encourage you to build those skills first before offering up this last aspect of boot camp, the internal search for greater success.

Skeptics of Commission for Life have asked me whether this type of reward system creates an incentive for employees to spend all their time prospecting and ignore their core responsibilities. In the ten-plus years I have run the program I can confidently say that I have never experienced that behavior. But I do believe that the message needs to be balanced to remind people of their primary job, and that doing great work and "intrapreneuring"—or opportunity spotting within the context of doing great work for clients—is extraordinarily valuable.

Open by letting your audience know that in this workshop, you'll be focusing on a slightly different set of skills. Here's how I begin:

> t is time to balance the message. Lead generation is terrific, but there are more ways to contribute to the bottom line of a business than generating new opportunities. In addition, in any business, it is important to ensure that client retention and customer service are your first priority. That is the art of being a great intrapreneur—nurturing your existing business to its highest return. In this workshop, growing from the inside will be our focus.

Content for this workshop should remain focused on the internal opportunities that can be spotted and exploited. You should cover the following content:

Being a constant source of great new ideas for existing clients. Remind your staff that it's not useful to wait until the client has an idea. Part of our job is to be that idea source. I have always felt strongly that great ideas find funding. Even in the roughest of economies, if you have the right idea, clients will find the money. As I write this book we are experiencing perhaps the most severe economic downturn of my career. And despite the budget cuts and client losses, great ideas are still finding funding within our client roster. Remind staffers that if they've established a relationship based on great work and trust over time, clients and customers will be open to expanding responsibilities and to funding that irresistibly great idea.

Knowing the company products and services offerings inside and out. Staffers should never miss an opportunity to cross-sell. The way to make that happen is for them to be fully conversant in what the company has to offer at all times. Encourage them to avoid putting on blinders and only worrying about their little corner of the company. They should be involved in what others in the firm are working on and how they can be of service to your client.

Being ready to respond. School staffers in the art of listening for clues. There are times when a client will drop a very important nugget of news, and staffers need to be ready to respond. The client may not spell it out—"I need someone to update my website"—and in fact may not even realize the need him- or herself. But if staffers are poised to respond, they'll hear it. When the client starts carping about his or her underpowered website, the staffer should be ready to respond with a proposal on what the company can do to help.

GROUP EXERCISE. Break into groups of four or five and brainstorm for ways to generate additional business from existing clients.

HOMEWORK. Each staffer should generate three new ideas for current clients.

The Employee-Eye View

How do the workshops work? Here's what some CJP employees told us:

What the workshops get you to understand is that new business doesn't have to mean cold calling. It can mean just keeping the idea of looking for new business in your mind. It's not about being pushy or aggressive. Once I was at my fantasy football draft and talking to a friend of mine, someone I've known since college. Ordinarily, I would not have thought to talk about what I do in that kind of setting, but in this case I tried it. I asked him what he was doing and he said he just started working with this new firm. Again, ordinarily, I would have stopped there, said "that's great," and moved on. But coming out of the workshops, I took it another step. I started asking him more about the firm, more about what he does. And it turned out, his new firm was looking for a PR firm. So I was able to say, "We have this great group that specializes in your type of company. I'll set you up with our person over there." It's not how I would have normally spent my time talking at my fantasy football draft. But the workshops had gotten me thinking about how I could do this, without being obnoxious but in a way that worked for everyone.

In another situation, I hosted a Fourth of July party at my house. There was a person there I didn't recognize, so I started up a conversation with him. He said he was a lawyer and did private equity work—a real mega-entrepreneurial type. So I said, "I'd love to meet with you and tell you about what we do." I did meet with him and a while later he called me and said, "I know some people starting a new business and you should expect a call from them." We signed that new business. And a year later they started another business and we worked with them on that. It was just a question of having that opportunity-spotting idea in the back of my mind. It made one conversation at a Fourth of July party into contracts for the firm and commissions for me.

—Josh, CJP

And here's how the workshop impacted someone just beginning his career.

I began as an intern at CJP. At one point during that summer, I attended a new business workshop. At the same time, I had spent some time picking the brain of one of our vice presidents about new business and prospecting. Following a great workshop and these conversations, I began to research financial institutions that I thought would complement CJP's already robust financial services client group. Being a student right outside of Boston, I focused my research on that region and began to hone in on one of the world's leading providers of financial services to institutional investors. I researched who the communications contacts at the company would be and developed an information packet about CJP to be mailed to them. Toward the end of my internship at CJP I mailed out the information and began trying to follow up. I did not reach the contacts while still at CJP, but from my dorm room at school I continued to call every other week until I reached one of the heads of corporate communication. She informed me that they had received the information and were thankful to have it and review it, but that the timing was not right. A couple of months later I received a call to my cell phone informing me that they'd like to have CJP come in for a meeting. As the story ends, we had a wonderful meeting and secured a project with the client that commenced almost simultaneously with my graduation and starting full-time with CJP. So in essence, I was a member of the Army of Entrepreneurs even before I graduated from college.

—Stephen

SIX STEPS FORWARD:

What to Do Right After You've Read This Chapter

Creating an ongoing system of workshops requires planning and organization.

1. Create an annual training calendar. Schedule all mandatory training events and be sure the information is well communicated to staff. Mark the time on your own calendar and be present. If you want everyone to take training seriously, be prepared to lead by example.

2. Create training materials well in advance to ensure quality. Ask presenters to submit their materials to you in advance for review and suggestions. Leave enough time for discussion and revision.

3. Create a system of feedback. Ask attendees to provide feedback on what they expected, what they learned, and their impressions of all workshops.

4. Measure for impact. What happens after a training session? Is there any discernible change in behavior? Why or why not? Ask managers to submit their impressions of how training impacts the staff.

5. Tap a training czar. Even if you will run the content of the training yourself, be sure you have support for the administrative tasks of training such as scheduling, securing space, and creating materials. Many CEO-led training programs sputter when the boss can't find the time to do the prep work.

6. Create your own training calendar. What skills will you learn in the coming year? Make a list and set times for your own course of study.

CHAPTER 6

Recruiting and Retaining Talent

I RARELY READ A RESUME FROM THE TOP DOWN.

Of course I'll look at the candidate's most recent employment line and scan his or her objectives section. But then my eyes drop down to the bottom. I'm looking for that first job or those early jobs. Often that's the nugget of information that's going to tell me if the person whose resume I'm holding is destined to be in my Army of Entrepreneurs.

If you took a look at the bottom of my resume, you'd see I bagged groceries when I was fifteen and clocked night and weekend shifts as a customer service rep later in high school. On the resume of my managing director, you'll see he once did weekend stints servicing the blast furnace of a steel mill. Another senior staffer at CJP worked collections for a credit card company. What do these early jobs tell you? They aren't glamorous or high-paying. They have little to do with our day-to-day mission at my firm. But they are important signposts for anyone hiring today. Those are hard jobs. They are "dirty" jobs. And the people who do them possess a certain kind of work ethic. A person who successfully works a dirty job as a youngster—and knows enough to leave it on the resume later—is a good candidate for the AOE. This is someone who knows about hard work and its rewards.

That's just one of the tricks I've picked up over the years that helps me hire and retain the right people for my Army. In this chapter, I'll address the topics of recruiting and retaining personnel. Any manager will tell you that recruiting is a huge challenge. But recruiting for an Army of Entrepreneurs is especially difficult. It requires a system of inquiry and investigation that will tell you not just about the skills an individual may possess, but about his or her inner personality traits that will suggest a successful future in an entrepreneurial environment.

It's not easy to find the right people for an Army. It takes a good bit of detective work and a willingness to do things differently. But when you've hired right, anything is possible.

Creating a Talent Pipeline

One way to hire smart is to never do it in a panic. This means creating and nurturing a constant pipeline of potential candidates. You may not need an individual right away, but you need to know that person now. Knowing who is out there and fostering an early relationship is the way you can make the right match at the right time.

Here's how to create a great pipeline:

Talent-spot constantly. Recruiting is not an event-driven task. It requires an ongoing commitment from senior leadership and a programmatic approach. You must see candidates as frequently as once a week to ensure a large enough pipeline of talent. A smart company will see twenty candidates for every one hire. When hiring for your AOE, that number can double. Why? Because you are now looking not just for those who have the talent and aptitude to perform the job, you are looking for people who might help you grow the company. That's a higher bar to clear and it will require a more rigorous and time-consuming review process. Assess your recruiting process and make sure it is active, ongoing, and forward-looking. You should be looking to identify candidates and get to know them over time, even before you have the job to offer. Never get caught in the trap of recruiting only when you need someone to start in two weeks. That's when you're vulnerable to making a mistake, overlooking a weak work ethic, or forgetting to sell the job. Event-driven recruiting is a risk to the organization and also brings down your potential for building an Army of Entrepreneurs.

Engage the staff in talent spotting. It was an eye-opener when I realized that I was not my firm's best talent spotter. I would have argued that point to the death. After all, I'm the leader; how can I not be the best talent spotter? But the truth is, I'm not. And I realized that after seeing the person in my firm who *is* the company's best talent spotter do his best work. It's important to open the talent-spotting process to the rest of the company. Encourage them by setting up a paid referral system for bringing in top talent. Your best talent spotter may be out there, just waiting for you to acknowledge his or her talents. Some companies take this process to extremes, offering far more than the standard four-figure bonus to an employee who brings in a key hire. Different companies may need different strategies to make this work. But it's critical that your staff members consider smart recruiting to be part of their jobs. Make it part of a manager's responsibilities. I make it a point to discuss recruiting issues in our weekly company blog so that everyone knows I consider it a priority and they should do the same. Too often, staffers assume that recruiting happens someplace away from the daily hum of the business, in some corner of the HR department. In fact, recruiting should have the same priority as marketing and new business. It is to everyone's benefit, and therefore it is everyone's job.

Be creative in job creation. One way to build a pipeline for full-time employees is to create ways for promising young staffers to get a taste of your company on a part-time basis. We have an ongoing system of internships that allows students to come and work for us. We offer training and credit and they give us a chance to train and "test drive" a potential hire. When I see someone who has entrepreneurial potential, we can make the effort to stay in touch and then reach out when a full-time slot opens. We make an effort to be creative in our internship offerings. For example, we aren't just a summer job. After all the summer interns went back to school, we created a full-time, ninety-day internship as a way to draw talent and come up with potential new hires for down the road. The person your firm may need desperately in two years may be halfway to her undergraduate degree right now. If you create a relationship, and you understand the other individual's personal and professional goals, you may be in a position to make a smart hire at the right time.

Don't hire only in flush times. Staff should not be an economic indicator for your firm—up when times are good and down when they're not. If that's the case at your company, you are missing the strategic element of staffing. It's not just about having enough warm bodies in the building to handle the workload. The right staff is what drives your company forward, and that's doubly important when the economy is struggling. Always be open to hiring the right person for the right job, even if the economics are not ideal. It may be the best move in the long run. I have often made strategy hires that at the time raised eyebrows. What's she doing? Hiring this high-priced talent in this economy? But I know what I'm doing. I'm making sure we are bringing in the talent we need to be successful.

Measure your results. Like any other effort, recruiting needs to be measured to determine what's effective and what's not. Edith Onderick-Harvey, founder and president of Change Dynamics Consulting, says that measurement of recruiting allows you to create a return on investment on your efforts and to adjust when something is not working as planned. "As the saying goes, you get what you measure."[1]

The Interview

When you begin the process of interviewing, don't do it alone. Involve other members of your team. This will help you get a full picture of the candidate. One individual might miss clues that signal yes or no, but a team will be able to pool its impressions and make a smarter decision.

Managers are not the only ones who benefit when the interview is a team process. Staffers know better than anyone that a great hire will make their jobs easier and a poor one will make everyone miserable. By including others in the recruiting process, you make it more likely that the new hire will mesh well with the staff. After all, staff helped make the hire. And finally, when more people are involved in the hire, more have a stake in helping that new hire become successful.

The key to successful team interviewing is a consistent, articulated strategy. Too often, interviews fail to turn up great candidates because interviewers are left to their own devices when it comes to developing probing questions. This leads to all kinds of problems, say Geoff Smart and Randy Street, coauthors of *Who: The A Method for Hiring*. Interviewers end up creating their own systems for evaluating candidates, such as the Art Critic (someone who uses a "gut" feeling to decide whether or not he or she likes a candidate) or the Trickster (an interviewer who uses trick questions designed to trip up the candidate). Often these ad hoc systems make everyone feel like they are interviewing properly, but they are actually muddying the waters, making it more difficult for a company to spot the right candidate for the job. What does a company really need?

A company needs key tools to move ahead with confidence and clarity. Those involved in hiring need a scorecard, say Smart and Street. This is not a one-paragraph description of the job. Instead, a scorecard must contain a concrete list of skills an individual would need to be successful in the position. Remember, it's not a list of what you hope the candidate will bring, but a series of must-see elements in the candidate you approve.

A company also needs good sources. Part of building your pipeline is reaching out to potential sources and creating relationships that will allow you to tap new talent when you need it, they say.

Finally, they say, smart companies need a real selection process. A structured interview process is what dissuades managers from coming up with their own methodologies for screening candidates.[2]

This is what we make sure is included in the CJP process:

Motivational synergies. What are you looking for in an interview? Most make the mistake of interviewing for skills. My advice is that it is easy enough to find out what skills a person has. What you want to do in the interview process is probe for the more important, less obvious elements that will lead to success or failure. In their new book *Identity Economics*, George Akerlof and Rachael Kranton say that a successful economy is driven by workers committed to their activities, much the way soldiers might be committed to their cause. We all understand instinctively that people will make major sacrifices for a cause they believe in. This human motivation is tapped by military leaders, who need soldiers to display that sort of commitment. But business, the authors believe, fails to provide civilian workers with that same sense of cause and commitment. The result is an undermotivated workforce. I believe managers can counteract that lack of commitment as early as the interviewing process. Probe for what the candidate is committed to—not just the skills he or she has learned, but what the candidate cares about, what he or she would sacrifice blood, sweat, and tears to achieve. And when you hear that commitment, ask yourself, is that in line with what we as a company are committed to here? Is there a motivational synergy here?

Work ethic. I mentioned the "dirty job" litmus test earlier. That's just one way to find out just how hard this individual is willing to work at being a success. As the employer trying to engage and empower individuals to grow their careers and the bottom line of the company, you need to identify hard workers. There is just no substitute for a work ethic. At my company, one commonality among our folks is that we all work hard. Hard work doesn't have to mean putting in twelve-plus-hour days, but in general we all have a deep commitment to getting the job done. And there is no doubt in my mind that you can spot a work ethic in the interview process. Whether the candidate worked his or her way through college, or had the support of well-to-do parents but also chose to launch a business, work ethic is something you can spot. Pay attention to the little things and ask the not-so-obvious questions. If the candidate is from far away, ask how he or she got to the big city; maybe there is a story of commitment to be uncovered there. If the individual went to graduate school, ask why. What was the individual's vision for grad school? What did the individual think it would help achieve? You're looking for signs of vision, effort, goal setting, and achievement.

The Pitch

When you know you've spotted a good candidate, how can you get that person on board? My advice: Do it right and then not only will you land the candidate, but that person will stay with you.

Sell the job, not the company. You may have a great reputation, great training, culture, benefits, the whole package. But what you really need to sell at this juncture is the job. At CJP, making sure candidates have excellent skills comes first, but then we "sell the job" versus "selling the company." We make sure they understand the day-to-day position and what will make them successful. We lay out the expectations of the job. We detail our "Finder, Minder, Binder, Grinder" method of evaluation. In this way, we manage expectations. Nobody takes a job with us for the wrong reasons. This is often a challenge for the interviewer. When the hiring manager sees someone he or she knows will be great, the temptation is to sell sell sell the company as a fantastic workplace. But the key to hiring a successful AOE is full disclosure of the job requirements. Candidates have to know what they're getting into. Otherwise, they might arrive and find that entrepreneurial life is not for them. When that happens, everyone loses.

Be honest with yourself. You want this person. But can you make this person happy?

Probe candidates on why they are leaving their current employer and ask yourself whether you can deliver on the promise of a better job. Will your culture and the Army model make them happy? Do they want the added responsibilities that the Army model requires? Don't fall into the trap of hiring only to achieve your company's objectives. You need to hire to achieve the candidate's goals as well, whether they be financial, cultural, or skills-based. This is often a difficult adjustment for the interviewer, particularly if he or she is also the CEO. As CEOs, we are hard-wired to be thinking all the time about what is best for the company and what we can do to make the company more successful. To turn that around and think honestly about whether or not we can make another person happy in our company is a stretch. I can't imagine being happy anywhere else. But to make a smart hire, I have to put myself in that person's place and be honest with myself if the answer is no.

Have a variety of value propositions. It takes many types of people to make a company run. You may have a variety of needs from your recruiting process. You many need an Army of entry-level employees. You may need seasoned veterans. You may need financial skills, technical skills, marketing skills, or international experience. For that reason, you need to look at the way you are reaching out to your potential candidates. The reasons that brought you to your company may not be the same for them. What you find appealing and exhilarating may or may not be as attractive to an individual considering your firm as a place of employment. A *McKinsey Quarterly* survey found that companies around the world are most successful when they are able to see their own companies from a variety of perspectives. U.K. retailer Tesco created specialized sections of its website to appeal to different segments of its job candidate population: current students and those who have already graduated. The site content is tailored to meet the information needs of these different groups, understanding that no "one size fits all" communication strategy is appropriate. Multinationals such as General Electric and HSBC created recruiting materials tailored to the local economies. For example, in China, both firms emphasize opportunities for career development, housing, and real decision making, all elements that might not have the same impact on U.S. job seekers. These firms understand that part of successful recruiting is successful target marketing. It takes a wide variety of individuals to make a successful company hum. It stands to reason that it would take a variety of value propositions to attract that spectrum of individuals to your company.[3]

Leverage the reference check. The reference check is the secret weapon in hiring. Many managers make the incorrect assumption that reference lists are dominated by friends and fans who will sugarcoat the employee's performance record. Quite the contrary. It is my firm belief that recommending someone is a deeply personal decision and that most folks, when pressed with the right questions, will tell the truth about an employee's performance record. But you must ask the right questions to get the answers you need. One of my favorite questions is "When a great person leaves a company he or she leaves a hole to fill. What hole will this person leave when he or she exits the company?" Hesitation and bland answers tell you that the employee might be solid but not good enough to make an impact upon departure. Another terrific question is "I noticed this person is on the high end of her salary range. Do you think she is worth it?" These direct, probing questions leave little room for the disingenuous reference.

After the Hire

The tough job of recruiting isn't over when the offer is accepted. It just moves to the next stage: ensuring that new hire sticks.

Allow for an adjustment period. Your entry-level hires will be faster to embrace the Army model than those who are seasoned and experienced. Why? The new folks have few preconceived notions; they come like moldable clay, ready for anything. Your more senior hires will require time to adjust to the Army model, which can sometimes be dramatically different from their former environment. You need to understand the process of adaptation to your model and manage your own expectations. Junior hires will morph fast; senior hires will take six to twelve months in many cases. For this reason it is imperative, especially with senior hires, to "sell the job." Although the Army model will excite them because it is new and different and highly entrepreneurial, they need a high level of commitment to learning and adapting to be successful in it. We recently hired a vice president–level professional from a competitive agency. She has about twelve years of experience and is an extremely smart and capable professional. Immediately we could see a high level of skills competency when she began her job at CJP. But quickly we realized that she would be a "six monther." It turned out, after further probing, that her former employer, where she spent more than five years of her career, was so tight with information that she didn't even know the revenue figures associated with her account load, nor was she allowed to ask. As much as she is enjoying our flat structure and high level of information sharing, it is so alien to her that she needs time to adapt. Adaptation will happen with the right hires; it just takes time. Be prepared for it and don't panic. If you did your hiring right, this adjustment period will pass.

Be transparent with existing staff. One of the ways a new hire succeeds is when he or she is embraced by the existing staff. This doesn't always happen. At some companies, particularly those with vibrant, competitive cultures, employees can sometimes find it tough to trust the newcomer. One veteran shoe designer, who went from Adidas to work at Nike, spoke glowingly of his new company, its power and resources. But even after several years he wondered if his colleagues were ever going to stop referring to him as "the Adidas guy." One way to help a new hire adjust is to communicate to the existing staff how that person is going to fit into the company's mission. I've found this particularly important when making hires during lean times. When the economy is rocky, staffers are often highly sensitive to changes that might affect them or indicate their future worth to the firm. For example, if someone were hired at a time when the staff was being asked to cut back, that might stir up worried talk about resource management at the company. Or if someone were hired in a specific specialty, others with similar skills might worry about being replaced. The key to managing this natural human reaction is to talk about it. When I make a hire, I announce it. When I make a hire that might be controversial (such as during a tough economic period), I address that directly. I encourage people to talk to me about their concerns. I remind them that everything (short of other people's salaries) is available for discussion. Certainly, I think you can learn more when you ask direct questions than when you stand around the watercooler picking up tidbits of gossip.

Get feedback from the employee. Not only do we ask our new hires how they're doing, we also encourage them to share their experiences. Here's an excerpt from CJP's weekly company blog. We call it the *J Low Down*.

Notes from an Intern

As everyone knows, our internship program is vital to identifying future talent at CJP. We take it very seriously and always do our best to ensure that our interns have a great experience while at the firm. I am attaching a summary written by our recent intern, Marcella, about her experience working in the CT office. I was extremely proud to see the kind of quality experience we provide. Once again, a special shout out to Steve for his leadership.

The CJP Intern Experience by Marcella ("as told to Steve"):

As my first week of school draws to a close, I am reminded of the great impact my internship at CJP has made in such a short time. The skills I developed over my winter break are already putting themselves to good use in nearly all of my classroom assignments.

Design a public relations campaign for an investment firm? No sweat, thanks to the project I worked on with Jessica, or the media lists and scans I made with Steve. Discuss the challenges of cross-cultural communication? My work with Lauren on Media Training in Spanish, and my research with Susan, Dave and Eric on the communication within multi-national organizations have certainly given me the leg up on my CJP-less classmates.

I have been able to see how professionals address their clients' needs with a multi-faceted approach, whether it was from Jessie and Joe on a social-networking project or from Jill and Dawn on the Holiday Mail for Heroes campaign. In my short time, I had the opportunity to work on a variety of projects with a variety of people and that has truly made all the difference in what I've gained from this experience.

Through the CJP internship, I have had the opportunity to peer into the world of public relations and return with a fresher perspective on business and the media on the whole. I know this is integral not just to my success in school, but my achievement in future positions and beyond.

There are also less quantifiable things that I have gained since my time as an intern. The night before my big debut, I was nervous about what to expect in my first "real" internship. I liked that Steve outlined the types of projects I might be working on, but I was unsure of the office environment. What a relief to find that I was surrounded by considerate professionals that were willing to take me under their wing and let me take a stab at some of their projects. While some may doubt the effectiveness or productivity of a month internship, I think that by hitting the ground running I had the opportunity to learn faster, work harder, and ultimately really earn and enjoy the feelings of contribution and accomplishment.

My only wish is that I had more time in the office to work on projects. I know that I only scratched the surface of the different responsibilities of CJP employees and would have liked to explore other aspects of public relations in the Connecticut and New York offices.

It's an odd feeling to switch from real world business time to the slow-paced, isolated bubble of college. My time as an intern has been invaluable to what I now can offer as a future graduate and employee, and I can't shake the feeling that there's still work to be done. In the meantime, to avoid getting rusty, I guess I'll call reporters and set up bogus interviews on my own.

Marcella's post served two important recruiting-related purposes. First, it allowed us to hear from her what the experience was like at CJP. This positions us to better sell the company as we go out looking for new talent. It also helped me reinforce to the staff that internships are more than just an opportunity to secure warm bodies at a low price. This is part of our talent pipeline process, so much so that we asked her to write about her experiences for the full CJP audience.

Consider retention a business priority. The return on investment of retaining a stellar employee for a five-year period versus a one-year period is dramatic. It is not enough to have talented people flowing into your firm; you have to make them want to stay, integrate into your Army, and serve. That means part of your recruiting strategy must extend to what happens next.

Case Study: Randstad

Based in Holland, staffing firm Randstad faced a problem: how to get new hires to ramp up to successful participation quickly. In its case study on the firm, Bersin & Associates described how Randstad crafted a solution.[4]

The issue, the company decided, was not one of hiring but of what happened right after the hiring process closed, the period many companies call onboarding. Randstad created a four-month structured onboarding process with the following elements:

♦ **Manager-Facilitated Training.** Content included company culture and values, job expectations, sales-skills development, and performance and bonus plans. Information was delivered in two individual two-day courses and facilitated by the employee's district manager. New employees rated the quality of the instruction and the usefulness of the material to the job they had been hired to perform.

♦ **Instructor-Led Classes.** In-house "learning teams" taught these classes on topics such as operations and sales training. New employees signed up on their own. After the class, they were asked again to report on the relevance and effectiveness of the training provided.

♦ **Self-Study Programs.** Individuals were able to pursue learning at their own pace on topics related directly to the company's business such as use of the company database, the company's organizational structure, and resources available to staffers.

♦ **Job Shadowing.** This experiential training allowed new hires to look on as veteran employees and managers did their jobs.

♦ **Manager Coaching**. Armed with a worksheet of job expectations, the direct supervisor conducted a series of formal and informal feedback sessions with the new employee.

What happened? The results were dramatic. New hires undergoing the new onboarding program outperformed their colleagues significantly. For example, the rate of growth in the number of calls made by the trained employees was nearly four times the rate of those who did not receive the training.

This case study is not just about the value of training. I've made my point many times that I think training is critical. I include this case here to make an additional point. Building a talent pipeline is not just about getting warm bodies in the door. It's about making the hire work once the employee is on board.

SIX STEPS FORWARD:

What to Do Right After You've Read This Chapter

To hire the perfect employees, you need the perfect recruiting tools. Begin building your arsenal.

1. Create a list of key attributes of the ideal AOE employee. Circulate so that the rest of the staff can be your eyes and ears in the marketplace; you may not always be in a position to spot the perfect hire, but another staffer may have that opportunity.

2. Create a list of interview questions and circulate it to managers. Make sure your interviewing process is coherent and organized.

3. Create a recruiting schedule. List key events you will attend and specific times you will put recruiting at the top of your to-do list.

4. List your five recruiting goals for the coming year, two years, and five years.

5. List five new places you will extend your recruiting efforts in the coming year. A wide net offers the best opportunities for hiring success.

6. Tap a recruiting czar. This may be your human resources manager or another individual in the firm. This is the point person who should not only spearhead recruiting, but also be the collection point for information regarding recruiting issues. Too often, great ideas surrounding hiring sit untapped at the staffer level because the individual doesn't know what to do with the tidbit of information. Tap an individual in your management ranks and let everyone know that this is who to come to with information or suggestions regarding recruiting. Then, when your intern overhears the news that a star player may be ready to seek a new job, she'll know where to go with the information.

Notes

1. Edith Onderick-Harvey, "Building Sustainable Talent Pipelines," American Management Association, February 2008. http://www.amanet.org/training/articles/Building-Sustainable-Talent-Pipelines.aspx.

2. Geoff Smart and Randy Street, *Who: The A Method for Hiring,* 1st ed. (Ballantine Books, 2008).

3. Matthew Guthridge, Asmus B. Komm, and Emily Lawson, "Making Talent a Strategic Priority," *McKinsey Quarterly,* January 2008. https://www.mckinsey quarterly.com/Organization/Talent/Making_talent_a_strategic_priority_2092.

4. Karen O'Leonard, "Onboarding at Randstad: Reducing New Hire Time to Competency," August 2005, http://www.bersin.com/Lib/Rs/Details.aspx?-Docid = 10335284.

CHAPTER 7

Using Technology

I BEGAN WRITING THIS CHAPTER STARING INTO THE SCREEN OF MY
Blackberry. I considered the topic of the chapter, opened my mind,
and let my thoughts pour out through my thumbs onto the mini-
page. Those were the notes that would eventually become the text
you're reading now.

If you had told me ten years ago I'd be writing the first draft of
my book with my thumbs on a two-inch screen, I would have
laughed. But times have changed and technology has propelled us
into a brave new world. The truth is, if I had to wait until I had time
to clear my schedule, sit down at my desk, and write as I'd been
taught in grade school, these pages would never have made it out of
my head. Technology made this book possible. And I'm not surprised
by that because technology is responsible for many of the successes
that take place within an AOE.

The Army of Entrepreneurs is a wired operation. We require a
great deal of speed and flexibility from our troops, and there's little
chance that could happen without the aid of technology. We use it

to communicate with each other, to communicate with our clients, and to understand the fast-moving business world around us. A recent survey found that Americans would sooner give up TV, alcohol, and even sex before they'd part with their cell phones.[1] They say this even while acknowledging that today's "smart phones" with e-mail and Internet access tie us ever more closely to our jobs. Entrepreneurs—in big and small firms—are not put off by that closer tie. Indeed, it is our ability to remain connected that often allows us to achieve our greatest business success. Certainly, the "always on" nature of technology is a boon to the AOE system.

In this chapter, I'll outline the ways technology is critical to the Army approach. I'll also discuss where I think technology could take us in the future. And perhaps most important, I'll let you in on where we *don't* use technology. Because as great as it is to be able to write a book with your thumbs at thirty thousand feet on a business flight to London, even technology has its limitations.

Technology as a Communications Strategy

I think it's important to begin our discussion with a definition of what I mean when I say technology. For the purposes of this chapter, I'm referring primarily to communications technology. If you're looking for recommendations on the best accounting software or news on whether CJP is a Mac or PC workplace, this is not where you'll find it. I'm not putting myself out as an expert in hardware, software, or anything in between. What I've learned is how the new technology in the communications universe supports the work of an AOE. It's been my experience running my own company and advising others that communications technology not only enhances entrepreneurial behavior, when used well it also becomes a critical point of differentiation. If I were to look at two companies, both with an AOE strategy, I could tell you which one was going to be more successful based on the implementation of communications technology. Technology, from my perspective, is all about the movement of information. I'll leave the advice about servers and routers to the IT experts.

For our business, the most critical use of technology revolves around our ability to communicate with one another. Certainly, we use all the standard-issue technology around e-mail and cell phones. But to make the Army hum, we take our use of technology up a notch and tap into new media options.

One of our primary tools is the blog. Once considered the digital equivalent of a teenager's diary, blogs have evolved into critical business tools. Nora Ganim Barnes, Ph.D., Chancellor Professor of Marketing at University of Massachusetts Dartmouth and author of the study *Behind the Scenes in the Blogosphere: Advice from Established Bloggers*, says blogging is the practice that allows business people to bust barriers. It may be the barrier a company faces as it enters a new global market. Or it may be the barrier a CEO faces when he or she attempts to communicate with his or her staff. But Dr. Barnes believes that the communicative properties of the blog lend themselves to this cross-barrier conversation and give the business person a way to move past hurdles. Executives may find this process daunting; it requires an investment of time, planning, and a willingness to engage in a more free-form give and take than most managers are used to. But, she says, it is vital to success in the modern marketplace.

"Blogs will make or break your business. They have the power to disseminate information and host global conversations on any topic. Every publication from *BusinessWeek*, *Forbes*, and the *Wall Street Journal* to online white papers from Marqui (www.marqui.com/blog) warns businesses that blogging is not an optional endeavor."[2]

But even with that news, some CEOs avoid blogging and other forms of social media. A study by UberCEO shows just how disconnected the most senior managers in our business community are. Of Fortune 100 CEOs:

♦ Only two CEOs have Twitter accounts.
♦ Only thirteen CEOs have LinkedIn profiles. What's more, of those only three have more than ten connections.
♦ Eighty-one percent of CEOs don't have a personal Facebook page.

♦ Three-quarters of these CEOs appear in a Wikipedia entry. But many of the entries have only limited or (worse) outdated information.[3]

These CEOs are missing a key value of technology in the workplace today. I believe that blogging is a critical technology option for an entrepreneurial company. It's both conversational and permanent. As such, it's a technological innovation in communications strategy. Former Sun Microsystems president Jonathan Schwartz wrote an article for *Harvard Business Review* about his experiences called "If You Want to Lead, Blog." Among his observations:

"Blogging lets you participate in communities you want to cultivate—whether it's your employees, potential employees, customers or anyone else—and leverage your corporate culture competitively."[4]

I agree. Here's how we do it at CJP:

The internal blog. Once a week in our firm everyone is invited to read the latest postings of my blog, the *J Low Down*. Started in 2008, the *J Low Down* is my way of communicating to the staff what is happening with the company, what I need to see from them going forward, and what many of them are already doing well that deserves kudos or a shout-out from the boss.

The blog often begins with my thoughts on the week's events. I've removed the names—we're strict about confidentiality—but here's one example:

We are off to the races at CJP into 2010 and the feeling of "opportunity" is in the air. I'm not sure I've had a week with as many quality meetings as last week. Among highlights was our pitch to [Company A] and [Company B], lunch with [Company C], head of comms, pitch to [Company D] and pitch to [Company E], and the list goes on. The IR team also submitted their response to a monster RFP last week (fingers crossed).

That's a typical way I run down the week's events—highlights, challenges, a kudo or two. But it's important to me that this blog not be The World According to Jen, because that's not helping to engage and motivate the staff. So another running feature of the *J Low Down* is all about what's going on in the business. It may be a recitation of clients won (and lost) in recent weeks. It may revolve around a business trend that is affecting us or our clients or both. Here's an example of that:

Did You Know That About CJP?

One of our challenges as a firm is making sure we communicate all the resources and experiences of the place. There are far too many times when someone is surprised to find out all the things we do. Below are a few things that came across my radar screen in the past few weeks and months that are worth mentioning. If you want follow up information on any of them please ask!

Did you know????

♦ We had a cover story in *Private Wealth Manager* for [Company A] this week

♦ CJP ranked number 38 on the *PR Week* list of independent PR firms this week (and number 34 on the O'Dwyers list)

♦ We had an advertisement in this month's issue of *PR Week*

♦ We have a major corporate video assignment underway for [Company B] (builds our video portfolio)

♦ We are working on a Web site for commodities trading firm [Company C], and designed two advertisements this week (renaissance marketing is happening!)

♦ We are working with a consultant on a major market research project for [Company D] and are interviewing 125 CEOs to generate the data

♦ Our Easton Studio press book for [Company E] is about to publish with galley copies already available (see Emily for details)

I don't just limit my blog posts to good news, either. Here's one I would have preferred not to write:

O ver the past few weeks, a few more clients cut budgets. [Company A] cut its budget by almost 50% this week, [Company B] won its award and then cut the budget (thanks!), and [Company C] also made a "symbolic" cut. The continued cuts remind us that the economic environment remains tough for many of our clients and we need to continue to work hard (and we are!) to insulate ourselves.

Obviously, these are examples of ways I communicate with my staffers in order to motivate them. So where's the technology connection? I'd argue that delivering this kind of motivational information via a blog—rather than another less techno form of communication—is critical. A blog is a unique digital communication strategy. It carries with it the casual air of conversation. At the same time, it has some permanence, stored within the confines of a company computer. If I sent out a weekly memo—the old fashioned kind, on paper—would I achieve the same effect? I think not. Paper is decidedly old and out of date. Just the idea of getting a memo seems like it came out of the latest episode of *Mad Men*. My message would be undermined from the get-go because I was showing a lack of cutting-edge awareness.

More than that, a piece of paper is a static thing. You can't talk back to it. You can't forward it. Generally, there's no way to interact with it. You just read it and maybe recycle it. It offers no sense of conversation. It's more like an announcement over a PA system rather than an invitation to talk. It's a one-way conversation. Instead, I opt for a blog, which supports my overall communication strategy of encouraging give and take.

On the opposite end of that spectrum, suppose I didn't write my weekly missive at all. Suppose I did it all verbally, either by gathering the staff or by talking to groups or even walking around the office and speaking with members of our Army individually. Certainly that would be very interactive. But it would fall short on another front: Talk is impermanent. It's there for the moment you hear it, and then it's gone. A blog, on the other hand, can be stored, referred to, used as an archive for what we are going through as a company. It can be read to discover trends and mined for content to use in other contexts.

The external blog. At CJP, blogging is not just an internal affair. We also maintain a public blog, http://cleverwittyquick.com, to get the word of our work out to clients and potential clients. In our most recent updates, we added video interviews with our clients, Twitter feeds from a selection of our staffers, and a mobile version for readers who tend to see just about everything first on the small screen (like me, on my Blackberry!). While my internal blog is about motivation, my external blog is about marketing. And again, the use of technology in this process is critical. If I were to convey the same information in a printed fact sheet, or even on a static website, would it have the same impact? I think anything that appears static in today's business world sends the wrong message. My use of an external blog does more than communicate information about what's new at CJP. It communicates how we view technology, as a living, constantly evolving element of our company.

Technology as a Business Tool

Communicating is critical, but ultimately we need the Army of Entrepreneurs to move from conversation into action. Technology plays a critical role in the execution of the company's day-to-day efforts.

The importance of social networks. One of my constant challenges is to encourage staff members to use new technology to both generate new business and serve current clients. What technology do I push? That's a constantly evolving list. For entrepreneurial companies today, social networks play a huge role in success. I challenge my staff to use social networks to reach out to potential new clients as well as to execute the public relations work for current clients. I have tapped one of my managers to keep tabs on the latest social networking tools and measurement systems and to make use of our weekly internal blog to communicate the latest trends to the rest of the staff. Not only do we need to be skilled in using this new technology, we need to understand the changing landscape and the up-and-coming new products. Clients will rely on us to tell them what technology they need to use in the furtherance of their broader corporate goals. My philosophy in using technology for clients is this: You never know it all. There's always something new that you should be looking at. Keeping a technological edge means never standing still.

Project spotting. A full understanding of technology is a particularly good tool for the new business tactic I call "project spotting." This is the exercise of taking an existing client and developing a project they didn't know they needed. Often, smart understanding of new technology is what makes the project-spotting effort a success. One of our staffers was engaged in an investor relations project with a client. As part of that project, the staffer had to frequently visit the company's website, which he found clunky and hard to navigate. But, being technically savvy himself, he understood what fixes could improve the site and what expertise CJP had in-house to make those fixes a reality. Consequently, he was able to successfully propose the project to the client and expand our relationship with that firm.

This can be effective even for clients who don't present as "techno" types. We work with one rather old-fashioned client, a bank that has done little to stay current with the technological trends. This firm is so old school it doesn't even have a voice mail system. We knew this and so we did not push our digital efforts. But then one day the client brought it up. We were in a meeting and one of the company representatives asked our opinion of digital media. We quickly responded with a pitch for one of our key tech products, the digimentary (our term for mini online movies spotlighting a client's product or services.) This old-fashioned client *loved* the idea and asked for a proposal. It was an important lesson to us: Just because a client has not embraced technological elements doesn't mean it can never happen. We must remain on the cutting edge of technology so that we can help our clients be ready to do the same.

The value of technological sophistication. Finally, technological expertise is something an Army of Entrepreneurs can use as a marketing tool. CJP managers are frequently panelists on discussions of technology in the business world. It's a way for us to be out in the marketplace, sharing our knowledge with industry colleagues but also building our brand as thinkers in the technological space.

As an example, CJP executive Wilson has helped put our company on the map with his creative use of media and technology. Among his many accomplishments is IKEA's branded comedy series, *Easy to Assemble*. Wilson worked directly with series creator/producer Illeana Douglas as well as on all marketing, social media relations, distribution, and publicity for the show's second season. *Advertising Age* recently named the show one of the five best branded entertainment deals of 2009. With more than five million views and growing, *Easy to Assemble* is one of the most-watched branded web shows to date.

But Wilson doesn't end his technology skills with client work. He's also a frequent speaker on the topic. At a recent Consumer Electronics Show (CES) convention in Las Vegas, he was a speaker on two panels, "Monetizing Original Media: 5 Winning Business Models" and "Creative Convergence: Energizing Entertainment." In doing so, he leveraged his technical skills to market the CJP brand.

Wilson's work gets a lot of attention, but he's certainly not the only member of the team to leverage tech talk as a marketing move. One of our firm's Army members carefully worked our relationship with a professional association. She booked a CJP manager as a speaker at one of the organization's round-table discussions on digital media, and then parlayed that into an invitation to its private networking event. By positioning us as thought leaders in the digital space, she helped us secure potential new business. That's a good example of why technology plays a role not just as a tool, but as a way of thinking about business. Technological sophistication is an asset in the marketplace.

The Technology in Your Future

What should be on your technology to-do list if you are an AOE organization? One element every organization should consider is a customer relationship management (CRM) system. CRM is an information industry term for methodologies, software, and usually Internet capabilities that help an enterprise manage customer relationships in an organized way. CRM is a bit of a mystery to many entrepreneurs. In the early days of the dot-com era, it was the must-have tech item. Lots of companies, big and small, invested in CRM systems and were disappointed by the results. It seemed to be a never-ending cycle of unmet expectations.

But CRM has come a long way, and today's systems are significantly improved—and useful to an organization eager to empower its workers. A survey by CRMindustry.com found:

- ◆ 81 percent of respondents are happy with the overall performance of their CRM technology vendor
- ◆ 53 percent currently use an in-house CRM solution
- ◆ 58 percent report that their CRM implementation was done within the estimated budget

The majority of organizations (66 percent) responding to the CRMindustry.com survey had plans for additional CRM projects in the pipeline.[5]

What are they all doing with that technology? Many are using it as a communications tool, to connect with their customers and each other.

CRM can play a vital role in an AOE organization by creating a database of information. Who are your customers? How are they connected to one another? What can you learn from those relationships? What other opportunities do the connections offer? When an organization is small, you can rely on the conversations around the watercooler to spread that type of news. A chat between two employees may reveal that one client has a spouse working at a possible new client, or other such connections that can turn into business opportunities. But the larger the organization grows, the more technology can help continue that exchange of data. With a vital CRM system, an empowered Army need not wait around and wonder if there are ways to leverage current clients into new business. That information is available, and employees are able to access it and act on it.

Where Technology Doesn't Work

As with any good thing, technology has its limits. While we constantly strive to use new technologies, there are many lessons we learn along the way that illuminate the ways technology can trip us up.

Here's a story I love to tell. One spring day, I learned we had picked up two print advertising assignments from an existing client. I was surprised, since I knew the client had a separate advertising agency. What had made the client turn to us for this work? We asked the client, and he said, "When I called my ad agency, I got voice mail. When I called CJP, I got my account rep, who is very accessible. So I decided to give it to you."

That's a key example of how technology is great, but human contact is even better. Sometimes, even with all the wonderful technology tools available to us, the client wants to speak to a human being. He or she doesn't want to e-mail you or text you or leave you a voice mail message, but wants to make actual—not virtual—contact. I use that example to remind our staff not to use technology so much that it becomes a barrier between us and clients. Ultimately, client relationships are human relationships. We can't let our technology undermine that.

We also send frequent warnings out to our staff about the dangers technology can present in the seemingly innocuous process of casual communication. An offhand comment you make to your neighbor or fellow traveler might never do more than elicit a chuckle. The same comment made via technology—such as Twitter—can have a very different impact. The news is full of Twitter accidents. One that hit home with us in the public relations industry came when a senior PR person was traveling to meet with his big client, FedEx, in the company's hometown of Memphis. The PR was not enjoying his visit to Memphis, and made the mistake of sending out a tweet complaining about the town. By the time he arrived at his client's headquarters, the tweet was a full blown PR disaster. That little comment, made by one person to another, would mean very little. But with the boost of technology, that comment morphed into a business headache.

Twitter is not the only tech culprit. We had another techno headache in the PR world recently when a public relations company employee failed to secure her laptop properly. A family member accessed it and used the information to engage in insider trading—another reminder that technology is a tool that must be carefully managed.

When to Turn the Technology Off

I'll end this chapter with a brief discussion of the role of technology in our lives as people. When you run your company as an Army of Entrepreneurs, you expect great effort and great results. But you can't expect everyone to give everything up to advance the fortunes of the firm. That's unrealistic and it leads to burnout. So while I expect that the members of my Army will work hard, I also expect them to have a life. Sometimes, that means turning the technology off. I do that. When I have dinner with a friend or colleague, I won't answer the ring of my cell. I won't check my messages on my Blackberry. Because as much as I am attached to those little machines, I recognize that the world does not spin on technology alone. A successful life—both professional and personal—requires that we still relate to one another as human beings. Technology is a tool; it's not oxygen. Know when to use it and when to put it away.

Case Study: Intuit and the Online Video

As technology evolves and expands, it can be tempting to gravitate to the "next big thing" debuted at CES. But often the most powerful business results grow out of the melding of an old technology with a new one. This is clear in the experience of Intuit as it sought to expand its reach into the small-business marketplace.

The challenge the company faced was significant. Accounting—Intuit's flagship business—was not a topic often talked about by small-business owners. They were usually more concerned with client-facing activities such as marketing and sales. So to get Intuit in front of the small-business consumer, its marketing team looked for a combination of tactics. Among them it:

♦ Provided a full suite of free small-business products

♦ Held a competition for more than $300K in small-business grants

♦ Donated to several small-business organizations

And then came what I'll call the mashup tactic. Intuit tapped a relatively older technology, video. It created and launched a video story of real small-business owners and real customers and posted it to the company website. Now, two elements—video and online—were working in concert. To build interest, Intuit funneled content from the business grant applicants into the website. Nearly two thousand text-based, inspiring, useful, and funny stories from real small businesses were added; fifty finalists provided emotional, powerful, and creative video entries for the final phase of voting.

The results were excellent. The company reported:

♦ 1.3 million visits

♦ Approximately 2,000 stories, 30,000 ratings

♦ Conversion rate on par with transaction sites

♦ More than 400 million impressions

♦ 12 percent of total talk about Intuit, 90 percent positive[6]

That dovetails with much of the academic research around online behavior. For instance, research by Harvard Business School professor Mikolaj Jan Piskorski revealed that pictures are a powerful online draw.[7] More than two-thirds of what we do online involves pictures. So when Intuit gave the dramatic stories of the small-business world a visual hook, it boosted interest in the content.

The moral of the Intuit story is this: Not all great technology is new technology. Sometimes an old standby can do the trick when paired up with a new media platform.

SIX STEPS FORWARD:

What to Do Right After You've Read This Chapter

Map out your technology strategy by first determining your priorities.

1. List ways you currently use technology to communicate. Look at that list and consider ways that strategy can be expanded or replicated in other parts of the organization. For example, if you're using a blog in one department, can it be expanded or replicated for another area of the company? If the website is currently being used to get news to clients, can it be leveraged for other communications purposes? This exercise will help you get the most from your current tech efforts before you go investing in new ones.

2. List five technology priorities for your firm. What do you hope to see? A CRM system? An e-commerce program? An Internet advertising strategy? A telecommuting program?

3. List the five tech skills you expect your staff members to have at the ready. Then poll managers: Can all employees perform these skills? Should you add technology training to your workshop program?

4. Poll the staff: What technologies have they heard about, tried on their own time, seen the competition using, that might be useful for the Army of Entrepreneurs?

5. Connect with industry colleagues and other outside sources for ideas. Another firm may have pioneered a technology process you can copy or adapt for your own purposes.

6. List five times technology has hindered you or disappointed you in the past year. What can be done to avoid this type of tech bottleneck in the future? Are there places where technology is getting in the way of Army of Entrepreneurs functioning?

Notes

1. Best Buy mobile survey, May 2009.

2. Nora Ganim Barnes, *Behind the Scenes in the Blogosphere: Advice from Established Bloggers* (June 2008).

3. "CEOs and Social Media," UberCEO, June 2009.

4. Jonathan Schwartz, "If You Want to Lead, Blog," *Harvard Business Review*, 2005.

5. CRMindustry.com's 2008 Trends in Customer Relationship Management (CRM), http://www.crmindustry.com/industry_research/crmsurvey08.htm.

6. Kira Wampler, "Elevating the Conversation: Small Business United," Intuit, September 2009.

7. Sean Silverthorne, "Understanding Users of Social Networks," HBS Working Knowledge, September 2009.

CHAPTER 8

Measuring Success

IN THE LATE 1990s, IT WAS FASHIONABLE TO MEASURE A COM-
pany's performance in terms of its stock price. In fact, it was all anyone talked about. Networking events, conferences, and business
lunches were filled with discussions of IPOs and options. Young entrepreneurs were turning up on the cover of *Fortune* magazine. How
good were the companies they ran? Just look at the stock price. It
was the yardstick of the moment.

It didn't take long for that bubble to pop, and when it did, many
companies landed with a thud. It was a cold, hard education for some
of those young newcomers to the business world that measuring a
company's health solely on its stock price was risky business.

In this chapter, I'm going to focus on how to measure success.
Taking the lessons from the dot-com era, I'm going to discuss the
multiple measurement tactics necessary to assess the function of an
Army of Entrepreneurs. Just as you can't tell a company's health by
its stock price alone, you can't tell how your Army is doing by any
one measure. Understanding your success depends upon data from

a variety of sources. Some of them will be familiar to you. Some may seem unusual. But taken together, they are the tools that will tell you how you are doing, what you need to change, and how close you are to achieving your goals.

Deciding to Measure

The truth is that entrepreneurial thinkers often resist measurement. It feels too safe, too inside the lines. We are a tribe of doers, of risk takers. We don't sit back and navel-gaze. We get out there and we trust our gut instinct and we go for it. The whole concept of the "gut instinct" is part of our business success creed. Beyond entrepreneurialism, and throughout the ranks of the business world, we respect this gut instinct process. It's no accident that the title of Jack Welch's best-selling memoir is *Straight from the Gut.* That's the kind of no-nonsense action man we've come to worship in business.

With so much of that gut instinct worship washing through the business world, it's hard to make a case for measurement. Nobody writes glowing business books and magazine cover stories about the process of measurement. Gut instinct makes much better copy! But I'm starting this chapter by encouraging you to resist the urge to act like a cowboy in the marketplace and to be smart about measurement. Even swagger artists like Welch know that measurement is what allows us to make smart, data-centric decisions. A study by consulting firm IDC found that 37 percent of business decisions are made on "gut instinct." But at the same time, 98 percent of managers place business intelligence at the top of their organizational priorities.[1] Sure it's great if you guess right. But it's a lot better if you're not guessing and still right.

Humans have always turned to tools to help them make decisions. It's just that recently, those tools have emerged as mathematical theories and technological innovations. In ages past we consulted the stars, the gods, the shape of leaves in our tea, for indications on how we were doing and how we should proceed. Today, we gather data and consult artificial intelligence in hopes of seeing a clear path forward. The use of measurement tools is not an abandonment of the instinct. It's a recognition that even our best instincts are enhanced by information.

Certainly instinct is critical when it comes to making leaps of insight and innovation. Henry Ford once famously said that if he'd conducted market research, his customer base would have told him to produce a faster horse. It was Ford's willingness to go on instinct that changed the world.

But the opposing evidence is equally strong. In the *Harvard Business Review* article "A Brief History of Decision Making," coauthors Leigh Buchanan and Andrew O'Connell point to many instances in which instinct might have been tempered by some key information. They include:

♦ Michael Eisner's expensive launch of EuroDisney

♦ Fred Smith's support for untested ZapMail

♦ George Soros's appetite for risky Russian securities[2]

And there are many more less-celebrated cases. The moral of the story: Trust your instinct, but back it up with data. The way to get data out of your business is to measure it, not just once a year (or when things are going badly and you're not sure why) but all the time.

When to Measure

I envy those of you reading this and setting out to start an Army of Entrepreneurs. You can do the best type of measurement: the benchmark before the process gets under way. You are the ones who will best understand how you're doing, what isn't working, and what needs to change. For the rest of us, the benchmark is less clearly visible, but it is still the most important step in your measurement process. You have to give yourself a starting line if you are going to properly gauge your progress. If you don't mark a start and a finish, you will need to rely on—you guessed it—gut instinct.

What to Measure

The key to smart measurement is knowing what to measure. Your initial benchmark process needs to gather and assess your current metric systems. What do you currently measure? Most companies measure revenue and profits on an ongoing basis. What else are you collecting data on? Are you regularly surveying for client satisfaction? For employee engagement? Also, are there other less obvious measurement processes going on throughout the company? For example, are there awards given by different departments or managers? These are in and of themselves measurement processes; you should know about them and their history. These are the tools that will tell you where you are at the start of your process.

What follows is a list of elements that must be measured in an AOE environment. Alongside the traditional elements such as revenues and profits, be sure you are measuring each of them.

Pipeline growth. One of the key benefits of building an Army is your team's ability to generate new business. Going back to my early days at CJP, I felt that the burden of rainmaking was disproportionately on me. When I got smart and began training and empowering the staff to step up and seek out new business, I noticed a change in the pipeline, that is, the business that is not quite signed but headed in that direction. A business in the pipeline might be one you are courting but are not yet servicing.

Every business owner knows that a strong pipeline is the key to overall success; it helps guard against the feast/famine business cycle. A more robust pipeline is one of the first changes you should notice when you implement the AOE process. Set big goals for this segment: Look at the volume of business in your pipeline and expect it to double. If you're not seeing that kind of dramatic improvement, go back and see where the bottleneck is. Do you need to do more or better training? Is your staff fully buying your call for more independent action? More potential work in the pipeline is an early indicator of success in an AOE environment. As your staff begins to step up, you should quickly be able to see more deals in the works.

Product innovation. This is another area in which the boom should be quick and obvious. If you've been effective in your communication during training, your staff should be coming up with new ideas—new products—on a regular basis and with energy and enthusiasm. You should be able to see a swift uptick in the overall volume of new business ideas. Even after all these years in the Army mode, I am often surprised at how quickly our staff responds to a heartfelt call for innovation. Some of our best new ideas pop up at offsite meetings when managers get up in front of the staff and talk about the need for new products. I remember one offsite meeting in which we came up with an idea, a twist on an existing information product. We called it Daily Squeeze. One week after the meeting, one of the staffers had already sold it to a client as a discrete product.

New products are inspirational. But be careful when measuring this element. You're measuring the volume of good new ideas. Some will work, some will not, for a variety of reasons. But watch for the groundswell of ideas. If you're not seeing it, go back and do more training. Go back and be more forceful about what you want your staff to do. Go back and consider if you've hired the right kind of innovative thinkers for your current requirements. And consider how you yourself are reacting to the new ideas. Are you enthusiastic? Supportive? Or are you skeptical? Dismissive? Be sure you are giving the green light for innovation, in your words and your actions.

Assignment size. It's not all about new business, though. It's also about growing current business. One of the things an Army employee is taught to do is what I call "project spotting," coming up with new opportunities within a client assignment. At our firm, we benchmark the size of a client contract when it comes in, and then again one and two years later. Depending upon the size of that original business, we expect to see anywhere from a 10 percent to 50 percent growth in that client, year over year. If that's not happening, we look back at our project-spotting process.

It's a widely known fact in business that it's cheaper and easier to get a current customer to spend more than it is to go out and attract a new customer. That's as true in a business-to-business set-ting as it is in a business-to-customer setting. An Army of Entrepre-neurs should be thinking all the time of new ways to get the client to spend more.

Employee satisfaction. The Army model should improve employee satisfaction across the board. It may not be immediate; all change is hard, and often a company transitioning into a new way of function-ing has its share of turmoil and worries. That's to be expected. When you ask people to do something new, naturally you will stir up con-cerns. Any employee would naturally wonder: Will this be good for me? Will I be able to succeed in this system? And does the boss really mean it when he or she says be more proactive? What will happen if I try it and get smacked down? So don't be too quick to demand that the happiness index rise. However, over time, a higher level of em-ployee satisfaction should be visible to you. As more staffers come up with ideas, as more have success seeking out new business, you should start to see their satisfaction improve. People like to be valued and trusted, and the AOE system does that with gusto. It is the sys-tem by which company leaders turn to their staffs and empower them to step up and be great and be rewarded for that effort.

Research shows that most people want to feel that kind of respect and trust in their jobs. It's also been proven that this level of satisfac-tion directly impacts a company's financial health. A study by Wat-son Wyatt revealed that strong employee commitment leads to higher shareholder returns. What's more, the research found that em-ployee commitment may pay off even more for companies in bad times than in good. High-commitment companies outperformed low-commitment companies by 47 percent in Wyatt's 2000 study and by 200 percent in its 2002 study.[3] When you're measuring for em-ployee satisfaction, you're getting a preview of your firm's financial future.

Participation in Army activities. The AOE system opens up a new set of opportunities for staffers, and you need to keep tabs on how many of them take advantage of that change. It's not enough to keep track of the volume of new ideas. You need to be aware of how many of your staffers are offering them up. If you've got a great volume of new ideas and they're all coming from the same two staffers, you've got a bottleneck. It's like the teacher in the classroom who always sees the same hands raised. You want to bring in the others to participate too. Measure how many staff members are successfully project spotting, how many are coming up with ways to bring in new business and earn a Commission for Life.

Remember that it's not just the raw numbers that matter when measuring Army behavior. If you've got a lot of new business coming in, but it's all from one staffer, you've actually created a dangerous problem for the company. What would happen if that employee left? Or got hit by a bus? Or took maternity leave? Don't just count the dollars, count the bodies in the program. If it looks like you're not getting 100 percent participation, look for ways to encourage others to jump in the pool. Be sure to acknowledge those who are participating in Army activities. Praise their efforts and reward their successes. Don't keep it secret; that's a mistake many managers make when they reward someone. They keep news like raises and bonuses secret, the theory being that telling everyone might stoke jealousy. But the truth is that the way to encourage greater participation is to publicize the success stories.

Customer satisfaction. Those who are skeptical about the AOE method often say that it could lead to a drop in customer satisfaction—that employees, focused on getting new business and Commissions for Life, will neglect current clients. We certainly haven't found that at CJP, but I acknowledge that it could possibly occur. The way to keep it from happening is to measure client satisfaction. It should stay the same or increase under the AOE model. If it drops, you know you've got a problem: Staffers are too focused on entrepreneurial pursuits and they're neglecting their "day" jobs.

The problem, though, is not in the Army model, but in the way you've communicated it to your staff. They need to know that customer satisfaction and a job well done are the top priorities. If your staff seems to be missing this, check your messaging. It's your job to be clear about what you expect from your team.

Tools for Measurement

In today's business environment, it's popular to rely on technological tools for measurement. But not every piece of data can be gathered virtually. The measurement toolbox must contain a combination of technological and human strategies.

Customer relationship management. A customer relationship management (CRM) system that gathers information from customers and analyzes for trends and trouble is an invaluable measurement tool. Once the tool only of large, well-capitalized companies, CRM has now evolved so that systems are available to smaller and growing firms. A CRM system can measure everything from the response to an individual marketing campaign to the impact of a new competitor in the industry.

Surveys. Technology today allows for the quick surveying of anyone with their fingers on the keyboard. Use the technology to connect with your employees, your customers, your vendors. Often these virtual check-ins will yield trends and valuable feedback. Be sure to offer a way for respondents to add comments—and read them. That may be where the real actionable data lies.

Formal gatherings. Schedule regular meetings with clients, vendors, and employees so you are constantly briefed on the status of your relationships and your progress.

Informal gatherings. Get out and talk to people. Encourage your staff to do the same. What a client won't share in a formal meeting, he or she may drop casually while having a cup of coffee with an account executive. Treat these meetings as important fact-finding missions.

Certainly they have a social function and they are valuable just for their bonding effects. But they can also be used to measure the health of a relationship or business process. Use them as a tool as well as a treat.

Outside Yardsticks

In addition to your own set of measurement tools, look to those on the outside to help you understand how you're doing and where you're headed.

Industry surveys can often give you a good picture of how well your Army is functioning. Recently we noted a major salary survey in our industry. While the survey said base salaries were down by double digits, at our own firm 95 percent of the staff had received a raise in the previous year. Not a big raise. And our senior managers took pay cuts to deal with the revenue downturn. But the vast majority of our staffers did not experience the slashing of compensation that occurred elsewhere in the industry. That's a crucial measurement element for our firm. It says that compared to other firms, we're doing well enough to continue to keep our employees whole. It says to our employees that this is a good place to work, that we value your effort, and that we won't throw you under the bus during a downturn. It says to our clients that we are smart enough to weather a downturn without resorting to tactics that would demoralize our talent.

Headhunters also make a good outside measurement force. They are keenly aware of trends in their industry, everything from compensation, to hiring, to trouble looming on the horizon. At CJP, we work with more than one headhunter in part to get a good understanding of what's going on outside our walls. The information they send back helps us know where we stand and where our AOE system is positioning us in the talent marketplace.

Awards programs are another way to measure how well you are doing. Look particularly for competitions that reward the kind of improvements you'd like to see. We look for contests that reward for business volume and for employee satisfaction, two yardsticks that are of particular interest to the success of the firm. Your company may have different priorities. Pick contests and awards that will push you toward your goals, not just pat you on the back for work you've already accomplished.

Informal Measurement

"Informal measurement" may sound a bit contradictory. After all, isn't measurement by nature a formal process? But I consider this particular form of measurement an important part of the mix, and I'll explain why.

Informal measurement is the process by which measurement is ingrained into the everyday activities of the firm without being a big, formal survey project. It is the way I make sure everyone understands that there are numbers that drive our business and that we are committed to them.

As an example, I offer up my weekly blog. The opening section of my weekly entry is almost always some discussion of a metric. Here's one:

t was a week of ups and downs, but the "ups" won out. Here are some highlights:

♦ (downs) [Company A] cut its budget by 10 percent but raved about the team. :)

♦ (ups) Tom, Vu, Brian S and I ROCKED the [Company B] pitch, last week. Accolades from the prospect were plentiful.

♦ (ups) Eric, Dawn, Sam and I charmed an ornery CEO. CEO said it was "the best pr presentation I've ever seen."

♦ (ups) Our ideas for [Company C] surrounding a major announcement, when compared with [our competitors], were far superior as noted by our client! Our plan is being submitted to corporate this week.

♦ (ups) Dawn and Tom rocked the [Company D] pitch.

♦ (ups) CJP/Cubitt are in the finals for [huge Company E]. Fingers, toes and bodies crossed. We should know in two weeks.

In that entry, I'm really not doing anything more complicated than cataloging the week's activities—counting the ups and the downs. Why? Because at times everyone starts to feel defeated, and when I can give them a metric to show them it's really not as bad as all that, the number helps me lead the Army forward.

Here's another:

'm not sure I've had a week with as many quality meetings as last week. Among highlights was our pitch to [Company A], lunch with [Company B] head of communications, pitch to [Company C] and pitch to [Company D], and the list goes on. The IR team also submitted their response to a monster RFP last week (fingers crossed).

That's not much more than a list of meetings, and meetings go on all the time, so why hold up a yardstick? In this case, I measured the week's meetings as a way to communicate to the staff that (1) the business was creating momentum, and (2) I liked what I saw.

Here's a final example:

As much as it was tough to do because of the awesome weather this weekend :), I personally worked on 3 different project proposals and one pitch deck for Monday! [Company A, B, C, and D!] This is very very good news per our offsite conversation about the need for summer projects. Thank you in advance for all the project spotting I know you'll all be doing this summer.

That's the most informal metric you can get: me looking at my day planner and saying what I did all week. But why do I bother to count the number of project proposals I was involved in? To use that number to communicate to the staff that this is the kind of behavior I want, that this is what I'm willing to do to move this company forward. This is what I want to see. I use the metric to lead by example.

I don't measure and report these same elements each week. What I do each week, however, is pick a number and highlight it. This is partly motivational; I often look for a number that shows how well we are doing. When I count and highlight the number of meetings in a week, it's to give recognition and support to the employees who acted in the AOE fashion and went out chasing new business. I cite that number to both thank them and motivate the rest of our staff. When I choose to highlight the wins/losses column, I am reminding the staff that we are all in this together, that the business I run is transparent and that they are capable of knowing and acting on the financials of this firm. Too often, companies act in paternalistic fashion and shield the real numbers from the rank and file. This leads staffers to come to their own conclusions about how the business is really doing—and they may be way off. When I choose one week to measure our wins and losses, I am reiterating to the staff my commitment to transparency and my devotion to treating them like smart, capable members of our team.

I may highlight a different number each week. But I always give them a number, a number to show them that measurement is ongoing, that the business is full of data they should want to know and use in planning their best and most productive course of action. You can call these numbers watercooler metrics; they aren't formal surveys or reports. They are the numbers I want to have everyone discussing around the office that week. They are the numbers that come up in conversation between staffers. It is a system of measurement that may look less formal than a survey or study. But it is still the appearance of a yardstick in the course of daily business, a reminder that metrics matter, all the time.

Analyze the Data

One of the biggest problems facing business today is the sheer volume of information and the great absence of knowledge. The Internet, for example, can overload us with particles of data. But can it make us smarter? That's the challenge. The same holds true when measuring the success of a business. It's relatively easy to get a lot of data, but much, much harder to make sense of it. This is a problem that vexes even the most experienced and successful managers. Back to Jack Welch for a moment:

"Too often we measure everything and understand nothing."[4]

One of the biggest problems facing any organization engaged in measurement is information overload. We experience this individually in the business world as our inboxes fill up and our phone messages go unreturned and papers seem to grow like weeds on our desks. We have more information than we know what to do with. This happens to organizations too.

In its 2009 white paper *Cutting the Clutter*, IDC researchers found:

♦ Workers spend more than a quarter of their time managing information overload.

♦ 40 percent of workers say they have the information they need less than 75 percent of the time.

♦ 60 percent of workers say information comes from too many different sources.

♦ 75 percent of workers say they suffer from information overload; of those, 45 percent said they were "overwhelmed."

When you look at the many ways information can come into an organization, it's clear why that happens. In addition to all the measurement tools I've already discussed, information comes into an organization via documents, forms, drawings, e-mails, instant messages, online formats, etc. IDC finds that 95 percent of the data flowing into an organization is unstructured, that is, not cataloged automatically. "This makes finding the right information at the right time incredibly difficult," the report stated.

I agree. So alongside a measurement policy, an Army of Entrepreneurs needs a way to catalog and analyze the data. Here's what the IDC experts recommend:

♦ **Digitize.** This allows information to be shared, read, diced, and analyzed without the time-consuming process of retyping it. In the Internet age, there's no excuse for data that's buried on someone's desk.

♦ **Centralize.** Everyone should know where to go when they want data. Conversely, everyone should know where to deposit data when they have it. This is one way in which the transparency of the Army is a benefit. In many organizations, information is closely guarded and not shared among departments. This "silo" mentality means there is no cross-departmental learning. A central information depository means information isn't hoarded and learning is shared.

♦ **Deputize.** Who is in charge of measurement and analysis? Be sure your staff members know what their individual responsibilities are in this regard. Do you want them to count client touches? Record meetings? Track e-mails? If there is a data element you want them to be responsible for, tell them early and often. At the same time, managers need to know their role in the measurement process. What are they counting? Who gets that information?[5]

Share the Data

Who should know about your measurement results? Everybody. This goes back to the transparency issues I've discussed earlier. To fully engage an Army of Entrepreneurs, you must teach them the business, and that means telling them how the company is doing. How are revenues and profits? What does the pipeline of new business look like? What new ideas are bubbling up from throughout the company? Who snagged a Commission for Life? Managers tend to regard measurement data as confidential, and there are certainly plenty of things you wouldn't want your competition to know. But some of this information—a lot of it, I'd argue—needs to get out to your staff. Knowledge makes staffers smarter. Knowledge of how their actions impact the company and their own bottom lines makes them more eager to work hard for the firm. When you work in a bubble and really don't know how you impact the process, it's hard to get excited about giving your all. But when you know you're part of a team effort that has boosted the company's performance, reflected well on you, and even put money in your pocket, you are going to feel more engaged.

You can share the information in a variety of ways. Certainly it can be done formally, in staff meetings, in annual gatherings, in press releases. But it can also be done more informally. I often share news that measures our performance in the weekly blog. As much as you as a manager might want to hide your faults and share only the good news, it's the sharing of information that brings the staff fully into the work of building the company. If you freeze them out, they are going to give you only the bare minimum. If you want the full effort, you need to bring them into the full experience of the company's process.

Case Study: Emerson Electric

There's an old saying in business: You get what you measure. That's certainly what Emerson Electric is hoping for under its new metric system designed to measure—and foster—groundbreaking innovation.

The manufacturer had set an ambitious goal: to make one-third of its sales from new products. The word went out to the company's sixty different business units. But how was that goal to be achieved? Senior management decided a new kind of metric was in order.

Emerson launched a new measurement system, one that came up with multiple ways to measure for innovation. It divided new product sales into four categories: minor improvements, major improvements, new lines of business for Emerson, and one final category called "new to the world"—truly groundbreaking ideas.

Under this system of measurement, an interesting trend was uncovered. Many divisions were spending far too much time, energy, and resources on innovations that fell into the "minor improvement" category. Upon seeing the numbers, a CEO of one of the business units was able to give clear directions to his team: free up manpower to chase the high-level, groundbreaking projects rather than make tweaks on existing products. The metric, he told *BusinessWeek* in an interview, gave his team the tools to go after projects that were "a little more difficult, a little riskier."

The measurement system allowed Emerson to see more clearly where it wanted to go and gave it the data it needed to secure more investment in its innovation goals.[6]

SIX STEPS FORWARD:

What to Do Right After You've Read This Chapter

Measurement is an activity that helps your business only if you knuckle down and get it done. Discussing measurement will not do much to boost your bottom line. But it is a complex topic. So here are some key first steps.

1. Review your current measurement tools. Ask staff members and managers to tell you what they informally measure and when they measure it.
2. Research new tools available to you. Are there technological tools you might consider useful to your metrics program going forward? Are there ways to tweak your existing technology to yield more data?
3. Review the research in your industry to see what others are doing and what best practices you may want to adopt.
4. Don't forget to consider low-tech as well as high-tech. Great metrics does not necessarily mean an expensive new software system. It may be as simple as an e-mail survey to a department or a show of hands at the next staff meeting. Focus on the information you want, and let that lead you to the tools you need.

5. Benchmark your process. All great measurement programs begin with the benchmarking. Know where you are before you can envision your path forward.

6. Ask for ideas. As with any new program, let all members of your staff know your goal and see if anyone has skills, background, or inspiration in that area. Your best metric idea may already be lurking in your existing staff.

Notes

1. IDC, *Taming Information Chaos*, November 2007.

2. Leigh Buchanan and Andrew O'Connell, "A Brief History of Decision Making," *Harvard Business Review*, January 2006.

3. Watson Wyatt, *WorkUSA 2002, Weathering the Storm: A Study of Employee Attitudes and Opinions*, September 2002.

4. Noel M. Tichy and Stratford Sherman, *Control Your Own Destiny or Someone Else Will*, 1st ed. (Doubleday Business, 1992).

5. IDC, *Cutting the Clutter*, 2009.

6. Brian Hindo, "Emerson Electric's Innovation Metrics," *BusinessWeek*, June 5, 2008.

CHAPTER 9

Officer Training

Every army needs officers.

As much as I promote and value independent thinking in my company, I know that a great company needs great leadership—at all levels. One of the key elements of success in an Army of Entrepreneurs organization is the selection and training of managers. These are the people who will be your voice as your company grows. They will be the ones to communicate every day to the staff the need for entrepreneurial thinking and action. They're the ones who will take your thinking and make it happen. Because managers play such a critical role in an Army, I'll devote this entire chapter to how to find them, how to train them, and how to keep them doing what they need to be doing so that the Army of Entrepreneurs is an ongoing reality.

How to Find Great Managers

The manager in an AOE is not like one in any other type of company. This individual has to do more than run a department and execute orders. An AOE manager is a rare breed; he or she must embody both the skills of a manager and the passion of an entrepreneur. That's not an easy combination to find. Most people tend toward one or the other of those two personalities. So how do you find the hybrid?

The answer I've found is that there are multiple sources for great managers, but no great manager comes with everything he or she needs to be successful. Instead you need to look for some critical core skills and then be willing to train and support the development of the rest. A commitment to officer training is the first step in amassing a strong manager team.

Knowing that you'll have to do some training, where do you find your best potential leaders?

In-house. For an AOE organization, the best source of leadership talent comes from within. My best managers are the ones who grew up organically inside CJP. They started in a variety of roles and with a variety of skill sets, but they emerged as believers in the Army method, and they stood out as stars in its execution.

That said, even managers who come up through your ranks will need the training that will make them leaders in your organization. We have seen that time and time again. One of our current managers, Doug, is a good example of this process. Doug was in his late twenties when he began to stand out as a star in the company. His entrepreneurial skills were off the charts. He was a whiz at attracting new clients to the firm. He had tremendous energy and was a strong player in developing new lines of business for the firm. Clearly he was someone we wanted to keep and tap as a leader in the company.

The problem was that for all his business savvy, Doug lacked the executive skills necessary to manage others, particularly in an environment like an Army of Entrepreneurs, which requires a secure and confident manager. But rather than wait until Doug gained more experience, we stepped in to train him for the role we wanted him to play.

This was *not* the path of least resistance. Doug himself was not wild about the idea that he had to change anything about the way he was working. He said (and he was not wrong about this) that he was bringing in a lot of revenue for the company, so why should he do anything differently?

We could also see it from his personal perspective: He was earning compensation far above his contemporaries. Why rock that boat?

My task as his manager was to help him see not just the present, but the future, for himself and for the company. Our task was to get him on a management training track, one that made clear the skills we wanted to see and the benefits that would come to him if he traveled this path. This was not a one-size-fits-all system, but a training program tailored to Doug. We knew he had the entrepreneurial skills to be a boon to our company in a manager role. We had to be willing to teach him the rest.

The key was intervening early, communicating candidly with the manager-candidate and not taking the "let's wait and see" attitude that senior managers often adopt when looking at junior-level recruits. Far too often, executives think they have all the time in the world to see how a potential manager develops. I think this is way off base. If you see an individual in your ranks who could one day move into a managerial role, you want to get him or her on track and make a commitment to that individual. The AOE approach is never about sitting back and waiting to see how something—or someone—develops. It's all about stepping up to the opportunity. In this case, Doug was an opportunity we were able to nurture into a win-win.

We had a similar experience with another organically grown manager, Kate. Kate emerged early as a star in a different way. She had terrific professional skills. She was top notch at counseling clients, managing crises, writing, and media work. She was a natural manager—all the things Doug was not. In any other organization, that would have been plenty to move Kate up the food chain and into senior management. But in an Army of Entrepreneurs, good management skills are not enough. Kate needed a strong dose of what came to Doug naturally—the entrepreneurial zeal.

The truth is, to manage staff members in an AOE environment, you have to be able to coach them in the entrepreneurial game. Many times, it is hard to pick up the phone and cold call, to spot projects in a cranky client, to reach out and network aggressively and effectively. When it's hard for staffers to do this, they need to be able to rely on their managers to help them through it and push them forward. So Kate was rapidly approaching a ceiling to her success at our firm. If she could not lead by example in the entrepreneurial space, she could not manage here.

For Kate, this was a frustrating situation. She was clearly good at some of the "Finder, Minder, Binder, Grinder" skills we needed at the company. But others were less developed. This was leading her not to the success she expected, but to a dead end.

As we did with Doug, we created a tailored training program. We knew she had the potential to be a great manager here, and we were willing to invest in her, to train her in the rest of the skills she'd need to succeed. We had her shadow other individuals involved in the new business process, and we chose "low-hanging fruit" opportunities for her to spearhead to give her some early wins as well as a taste for the success that work brings. The results were dramatic; Kate is one of our most successful officers and she inspires her team on a daily basis.

Kate and Doug are good reminders to me as I expand my company that my best officers may be right here and in need of a specially tailored officer training program. If I'm willing to look hard at what they can and can't do, and step up to fill those skills gaps, we are all the winners.

From outside. Not every officer can come from inside the ranks, especially at a company in growth mode. The development of the human beings within the organization just can't be fast enough. For that reason, every Army of Entrepreneurs needs a strategy to recruit managers from the outside. That's actually much harder than finding officer candidates from inside your company. For many, that's a counterintuitive thought; surely it's easier to go out and poach someone else's great manager? But the truth is that finding a manager outside your company who can come in and be a fit in the AOE is harder than it looks.

It's very easy to get burned by the great resume, what I call the bio trap. That's the individual who looks so experienced, so talented, that you're lulled into a belief that this person can do anything. Being an officer in an Army of Entrepreneurs is *not* something any experienced manager can do. It takes a special collection of skills and personal attributes to make the transition. So how can you hire? Consider the following key elements:

♦ **Culture Fit**: We've discussed this issue—the importance of creating a culture and hiring to fit that goal—in other chapters. This is tremendously important when hiring managers from outside your company to come in and lead existing teams. In order to preserve the continuity of your mission, you have to be sure this new individual has an active desire to work in a company like yours.

Probe this person during the interview process. What does this individual value in a corporate culture? What is he or she looking for in a corporate culture? What kinds of people would this person like to manage? Don't just ask the direct questions, either. Ask the questions that will get your candidate to spill his or her stories. For example, ask about an experience that helped the individual develop his or her managerial style. A culture fit is critical. Remember that this is a person who will be asked to supervise and teach others. If he or she is not on board with your culture goals, that will impair the management process going forward. Use this opportunity to emphasize how important culture is in your company. Many businesses just pay lip service to this goal. An AOE is more committed to living its goal every day.

♦ **Entrepreneurial Skills**: A manager needs to have both a passion and a track record for entrepreneurial thinking. If this person is not an idea generator, not a magnet for new business, not an opportunity spotter, how can he or she inspire others to those goals? You can be generous in your definition of entrepreneurialism; an individual from a large company or a smaller organization can be equally qualified. Despite the belief that large companies are slow to adapt, you can certainly find individuals with big-company experience who are new-idea machines, constantly on the hunt for the next opportunity. But you absolutely want your potential manager to both be good at entrepreneurial thinking and to love it. It's the taste for the experience that often drives people forward.

♦ **Teachability**: No matter how good the culture fit, how strong the entrepreneurial drive, you must see in your potential manager the willingness to learn. Why? Because a manager who comes to you from the outside has likely never worked at a company like yours before. The AOE concept may get a lot of discussion, but few companies practice it with consistency. That means most managers you recruit from the outside will have spent ten or fifteen years in a very different work environment. They will not have been schooled in project spotting, in drumming up new business constantly, in being proactive all the time. And they have probably not been taught to push those under their command to act independently, think proactively, take risks, and be entrepreneurial.

In fact, most organizations teach their managers to do the opposite, to manage and maintain control. So you are looking into your candidate's ability—and willingness—to learn. Is this person open to learning new ways of thinking? New ways of interacting day to day with direct reports? New ways of defining success? This will be the critical skill that will allow an outsider to come in, fit in, and lead others forward.

You may be surprised where you will spot this "teachability" factor. It's not always in the candidates you may imagine. We have a successful manager at our firm with a background dominated by service in the United States Marine Corps. You might be tempted to assume this person would lean heavily on his structured, hierarchical training to get a job done. But in fact, he was eminently teachable to the AOE way of managing, and his work successfully combines his military experience with an entrepreneurial outlook.

Similar to hiring at any other level in the firm, remember to hire for managers in a structured way. Have more than one person interview the candidate. Coordinate questions and discuss as a team what you're seeking. Remember to not be blown away by the resume or other sales documents the candidate may produce; take the time to go deeper. Most important to this and any other hiring process is the reference check. Do not be satisfied with the perfunctory recitation of dates of service and job titles. You need to ask real questions of the individual's references, most especially in a management candidate who will be called upon to adapt to your organization and lead others forward. Set aside time in your hiring process to do this part of the investigation properly.

From the top drawer. Wherever your managers may come to you from, it's important that they come to you from a place of excellence. Perhaps the greatest predictor of successful team leadership is success itself. A study produced by the Cornell University ILR School found a direct link between individual technical success and later leadership success. The three professors in the study looked at a unique group of workers and managers, the coaches and players in the National Basketball Association. By analyzing the data from the sports organization over an eight-year period, the study showed clearly that great players make the best coaches. The best predictor of success as a coach was clear—star quality success as a player. This result, the authors state, can well be applied to leadership in a corporate setting. What makes a great team leader? Who grows up to be the most successful manager? More often than not, it is the individual who is truly successful and a star in his or her technical specialty as a young worker. Why is this? The study suggests:

♦ Great players have deep knowledge of the game. This is true whether the playing field is a basketball court or a boardroom. When leaders come from a background of significant technical expertise, they are able to "see" the game in ways that less successful individuals cannot.

♦ Great players make credible leaders. A manager who comes to a team with a history of individual success will command respect and attention from the junior staffers.

♦ Great players signal a serious company. When a company makes the move to hire or promote a successful individual into management, that is more than an internal operation. It is also an external signal—to the competition, to clients—that the company is serious about building strong leaders. That atmosphere of commitment is a strong predictor of manager success.[1]

What to Ask of Managers

Once you have your managers in place, what do you want from them? Managers don't run on autopilot, even ones with talent and experience. To get the most out of your Army, you need to send your managers out with marching orders. As much as you give them freedom and responsibility, you need to be sure they understand the core cultural underpinnings of the organization. Asking everyone to behave in an entrepreneurial manner does not mean letting managers make it up as they go along. There are key factors that managers must embrace to be successful in an Army of Entrepreneurs.

Be a good boss. This sounds like a platitude but it isn't. The actions of being a good manager are definable. Bob Sutton, professor of management science and engineering at Stanford University, found there are evidence-based ways to be a good boss, even in tough times when managers may be called upon to do tough things such as cut budgets and staff. The key, he says, is to act in ways that both protect the company performance and preserve human dignity by being predictable, promoting understanding, being willing to give up some control, and being compassionate.[2]

Predictability is important for workers to make use of their own internal resources to handle bad news, Sutton says. Studies in humans and animals show that pain is less intense and easier to bear when it's not a surprise. Model managers let employees know when bad news is coming and when it's not. By creating an air of predictability, a manager can promote greater stretches of relative calm, even during a tumultuous business environment.

It's also a good boss's job to promote understanding, he says. It's not enough to say it once and assume the message has been heard. It's certainly not enough to send out a memo, or worse, an e-mail, and consider the job of communicating done. The goal is not just to express the information, but to act in such a way that staffers understand it. The AOE manager has to open the lines of communication to his or her direct reports and convey information repeatedly. Managers should subscribe to the constant communication process.

While it's not reasonable to turn the company over to the workforce, a good boss allows staffers to feel a sense of control. Staff members feel in control not only when they have freedom, but also when they are helped to see the best way forward in their work. In addition to fostering entrepreneurial spirit, an AOE manager must be willing to step up and help a staffer prioritize and focus on the critical goals.

Finally, says Sutton, a good boss must express compassion. Studies show that workers treated callously by their managers are more likely to steal from their companies. There is no reason, even in a tight and bruising economy, to lose sight of your compassion for your fellow human beings. Managers act as the voice of the company in the day-to-day activities of the firm. These are the individuals who will communicate your instructions and your values.

Understand the role of money. Money motivates many people. I've seen that happen with the Commission for Life compensation plan. Money also makes people happy. That came through in a study conducted by the University of Toronto and Stanford University. The research, spearheaded by Jeffrey Pfeffer at the Stanford School of Business, found a stronger tie between money and happiness for hourly workers, in part because they were better able to see the direct connection between their work and their compensation.[3]

This is an important goal as a manager in an Army of Entrepreneurs. Managers must help staffers make the connection between what they do and how they are compensated. They must continually promote the ways staffers can be in charge of their own financial destinies. In some firms, staffers have little to say about how much they are paid and what their earning potential is. In an AOE firm, that's not the case. But I've found that that needs to be repeated and re-emphasized so that everyone believes it. It's one thing for the CEO or owner to say that. It's additionally powerful to hear that message from your manager. For managers, this means more than just going over the company compensation policy, although that's good to do as well.

Managers must also continually recognize and promote those who are achieving success within the firm's financial framework. Has someone on the team secured a new client and earned a Commission for Life? Recognize, celebrate, and emphasize the opportunities for others to do the same. It's the role of a manager to keep that message alive in the day-to-day work of the staff. Too often, managers are schooled not to talk about money issues in a public way. I advocate a more open and transparent approach. Just as I talk about financial issues (with everything but individual salary figures available for inspection and discussion), I encourage managers to do the same within their groups. Money issues should not be secret.

Don't be a robot. There's good research to indicate that a little emotion on the job is a good thing. Professor Daniel Shapiro, a clinical psychologist and visiting professor at the MIT Sloan School of Management, found that the old-fashioned notion that emotions have no place in a corporate environment needs to be scrapped. In fact, expressing emotions can be a boon to a company and its workers. This is not to say people should throw their emotional filters to the wind and let it all hang out. But some emotions have a positive place in the successful firm, he says. These emotions are appreciation and autonomy.

"People will sacrifice a great amount for appreciation, and if they don't feel appreciated, they don't do a very good job. It's one of the primary reasons organizations falter," Shapiro says.[4]

Appreciation is a value we take to heart at CJP, and one that managers must continue to promote on the team level. Just as I look for ways to show my appreciation to the staff at large, I ask that managers do this on a more direct basis with their team members.

Autonomy on the job can be important as well. Says Shapiro, "None of us likes to be told what to do—not at home, not at work." This is another core principle of our firm that we ask our managers to practice on a daily basis. It's one that pervades the day-to-day life of a manager in an AOE firm. Here is how Todd, one of the managers in our firm, sees the process:

> I've learned over the years that you don't have to change every single thing that comes though the door. As long as there is a certain level of quality in the work, I let (the team) bring their own style to it. It inspires people, gives them confidence. You can't be the kind of manager who says just do it this way. You have to let them have some of the momentum.
>
> This means sometimes things are done in ways that I would not have done them. For example, I'm a very aggressive person. I feel like aggressive wins—a polished aggressive—and I'm the type to pick up the phone and cold call to get business. But not everyone is going to do it my way. In my group, they have the autonomy to find what works for them. If it's not a call and it's e-mail and that's what works for them, I let them do it their way.

What's another emotion with a place in the AOE experience? Anger. Not the uncontrolled kind, but the kind that is addressed and acknowledged with communication. Pretending no one ever gets angry isn't useful. Managers need permission to address unhappiness when it arises, not orders to suppress it and never mention it again.

Caroline, another CJP manager, speaks to this particular management challenge:

> The most important thing I've found is to listen to what they have to say. Let them vent and say what they are thinking. Then I'll

ask them, step back, and really look at this. Is this a justified response or are you being more emotional than you need to be about it? If this is a justified response, I'll go to bat for them. If it's emotion, I'm there to listen and to help them work it out.

Act as a Sponsor

There is nothing more demoralizing for an employee than to be told to come up with new ideas, and then encounter a brick wall from management. The Army of Entrepreneurs demands a constant flow of new ideas, and managers need to be ready to show support for the thinking as it filters its way through the organization.

In their research for Swiss business school IMD International, professors Peter Lorange and Bala Chakravarthy describe this role as critical to the fostering of entrepreneurship within an organization. They call this process "sponsorship" and describe the role as the link between senior executives and more junior staffers.

The sponsor, they say, is the one who can lobby for the lower-ranking individual's idea, give advice and support, and create the environment that encourages more entrepreneurial thinking. This kind of sponsor activity is common in Japanese companies, but firms in the West use it less often.[5] That's one of the reasons entrepreneurial managers often find themselves stifled at various stages of developing an innovative idea. Part of management's role is to create a structure by which ideas can bubble up. Part of a manager's job is to be sure that structure is working for all the members on his or her team.

Ultimately, the role of the manager is to act for you, the owner, when you can't be everywhere. To that end, this individual needs to be as steeped in the culture and goals of the company as you are. Managers in the CJP Army do not have an easy job; it is not simple to both lead and allow a level of freedom that fosters entrepreneurial thinking. Since we ask a lot of managers, it's important that we pick the right people for the job, teach them what they need to know, and communicate to them what we expect them to do day-to-day. Without them, the organization could not grow beyond one individual's ability to manage it. With them, growth is limitless.

Case Study: Innovation—It's a Management Discipline

Many people consider innovation to be the result of the free flow of ideas. But Esther Baldwin of Intel Corp is on a mission to reposition the idea of innovation as a management discipline. Baldwin launched the Innovation Center in Shanghai, China, and pushed to reposition innovation not as a happy accident, but as a task of every-day managers. Innovation, she says in an interview with *MIT Sloan Management Review*, is not about joyous brainstorming. It is the result of measurable, manageable activities. Her advice on how to manage for innovation:

♦ Use technology tools, such as databases, to capture employee ideas. Many companies have lots of ideas throughout the organization, but often there is no communication between silos such as marketing, finance, and R&D. Managers need to supply technology tools to support ideas and find them larger platforms throughout the company.

♦ Encourage employees to communicate with each other. A great idea isn't just something you bring to your direct supervisor and hope for the best. Use chat rooms, video conferencing, and social media to encourage greater sharing.

♦ Be prepared for initial resistance from traditional innovators. Oddly enough, when management steps up to support greater innovation, managers may experience some backlash, says Baldwin. There may be some in the firm used to taking the burden—and the credit—for innovation. Opening up this process to the rest of company may initially seem threatening to them. It's important to enlist these existing innovators in the expanded innovation process.[6]

SIX STEPS FORWARD:

What to Do Right After You've Read This Chapter

Creating a world-class management team is critical to the success of an Army of Entrepreneurs.

1. List the top three attributes of your ideal manager.
2. Review your manager training. Does it teach to these critical attributes?
3. List three in-house candidates for management training.
4. List three outside candidates for management.
5. Review three top competitors. How do their managers behave? Can any lessons be learned?
6. List three goals for your managers for the coming year.

Notes

1. Amanda H. Goodall, Lawrence M. Kahn, and Andrew J. Oswald, "Why Do Leaders Matter? The Role of Expert Knowledge," ILR Collection Working Papers, Cornell University ILR School, 2008.
2. David Orenstein, "How to Be a Good Boss in a Bad Economy," *Stanford Report*, June 3, 2009.
3. Christine Blackman, "Stanford Researcher: Money Makes People Happy, Especially If They're Paid by the Hour," *Stanford Report*, January 22, 2010.
4. "To Succeed in Business, Try Saying What You Feel, MIT Sloan Professor Advises," http://mitsloan.mit.edu/newsroom/2009-shapiro.php.
5. Peter Lorange and Bala Chakravarthy, "Are You a Frustrated Entrepreneurial Manager?" IMD Business School, Lausanne, Switzerland, June 2007.
6. "Innovation Isn't 'Creativity,' It's a Discipline You Manage," *MIT Sloan Management Review*, February 4, 2010.

CHAPTER 10

Maintaining Momentum

Whether you are building a business from scratch or revamping the process of an existing company, it seems at the start that everyone has energy to burn. But only the most novice entrepreneurs think that kind of momentum is self-sustaining. Those of us with any experience in the business world know that when the speeches are over, the memos have been distributed, and there are no more cookies in the conference room, many workplaces simply fall back into their old habits and nothing really changes. Existing companies slip into the familiar work patterns; new firms start to emulate their entrenched competition.

Of all the threats to the AOE process, this quiet slip into inertia is perhaps the most dangerous. It is the blow to the business that no one sees coming because it happens in slow motion. Over months, over years, champions of the new system lose their enthusiasm, and your company, once poised for a unique and powerful experience, slips into line with everybody else.

Clearly, falling in line with everyone else is no way to produce dramatic growth. So our challenge as business leaders is this: How can we maintain the momentum? It's one thing to come up with a good idea or to embrace a plan for improvement. It's quite another to find the process that keeps everyone motivated and moving forward—sticking with the program rather than letting it fall by the wayside. Most important, momentum is what helps great employees stick with you. When staffers can feel a company is going somewhere, they are willing to hang in and work hard to make it happen. A company that feels stagnant and stuck, on the other hand, is in danger of losing its best workers. Momentum is not just a way to keep a program on track; it's a critical strategy to keep your most talented individuals in your ranks and working hard.

In this chapter, I'll address ways I've found to keep the full-steam-ahead energy in the AOE process. I'll tell you up front, though, there is no magic bullet. There is, however, a web of activities and processes that combine to keep the energy level high. The three critical areas I will address here are compensation, morale, and communication. These are the linchpins to maintaining forward momentum. The key is to keep the idea alive on a daily basis and not let the program fizzle out before it's had a chance to succeed. You need your people to stick with you and stick with the program.

How to Pay So People Will Stay

I've discussed my philosophy around compensation in several chapters, but I'll review my concepts here and discuss why pay is so much more than money.

There are two basic types of compensation: traditional (cold, hard cash) and psychic (the elements of your job that may not be entirely tangible but have a huge impact on how you feel about your work life). Both are vital to maintaining momentum. Both play critical roles in motivating and sustaining an Army of Entrepreneurs. In this section, I'll examine both types of compensation and explain why both must be present to ensure a stable, motivated workforce.

Traditional compensation. Traditional compensation can take the form of money or other tangible incentives. A study led by Richard E. Clark, a professor of educational psychology and technology at the University of Southern California, found that traditional compensation in the form of financial incentives could have a dramatic impact on team and individual performances. He discovered that incentive programs improve performance by an average of 22 percent for an individual and as much as 44 percent for a team. He also found that incentive programs boost engagement. Workers who have a way to make more money show more interest in their work. Programs that have rewarded employees for task completion, persistence toward a goal, and "thinking smarter" have all resulted in improved performance numbers.

Clark's study further showed that incentive programs attract quality workers. Word gets around in the marketplace. Stars know which companies reward star behavior. If you've got a generous incentive program in place, chances are good it's well known both inside and outside your company. This is true for both executives and rank-and-file recruits, since both classes of workers report they value incentives.

Finally, when it comes to incentive programs, Clark advises: Take a long view. Long-term programs outperform short-term programs. The most effective incentive programs extend for a year or more. The study found long-term incentive programs produced an average of 44 percent performance improvement, whereas programs of a week or less yielded a 20 percent boost.[1]

My experience with traditional compensation programs has been that their successful implementation relies on several key elements. The first is strategy; compensation can't just be something you do to keep people in their seats. Compensation needs to be a system by which you motivate, train, and inspire. Be sure when you set up your compensation system that you are paying for the type of behavior that benefits your business. This sounds obvious, but in many workplaces it's just not the case. It's common, for example, to find a compensation system that rewards for years of service. To my way of thinking, that's a system that rewards an employee for holding still and staying out of trouble, and there's not much benefit to the company in that behavior.

Payday can be a critical time to communicate with your employees about what's important to the organization as a whole. When you look at the way you pay people, ask yourself: Are we using the paycheck to clearly communicate what we want and what we will reward? The best way to get the behavior you want from any employee is to tie it directly to compensation. As I found in CJP's Commission for Life system, when we wanted our team to work harder to generate new business, they were motivated by tying a tangible compensation system to the behavior we wanted to see. The results were quick and dramatic. What's more, the way we pay out the Commission for Life moneys is also part of our strategy. No one gets that payment automatically; it comes each month upon the collection of a bill. If the client doesn't pay, the commission is held up. We've found that this an effective way to educate the workforce on the challenges of receivables and collections. Everyone who seeks a Commission for Life in this firm also gets a strong education in how a business works. Employees who know how the business works are more efficient in their own efforts.

In addition to being clear, a good compensation system must be bold and creative. At our company, we want excellence. We want radically better performance. To that end, we offer market salaries—sometimes better. If you want the best, you have to demonstrate in the traditional income category that you are willing to pay for it. If you demand excellence but offer only mediocre salaries, that disconnect will be apparent.

Alternate pay forms can be effective as well. Certainly, executing a job well and routinely should be a way to earn money. But I've found that if you offer an additional option, you get additional effort. The Commission for Life and other programs that allow employees to pad their own paychecks are ongoing motivational systems. Be on the lookout for ways you can offer additional compensation.

Finally, don't let the naysayers get you down. I've had many people tell me that my method of compensation would encourage employees to devote too much time to new business and not enough time to existing client care. That's not been my experience. Giving employees a new way to make money motivates them to work harder for you in all aspects of their jobs. Be sure you couple your compensation opportunities with strong education on how the company works. When employees know how to make money—for themselves and for the firm—they step up.

Psychic compensation. Where traditional compensation leaves off, psychic compensation picks up. Psychic compensation is that which is not money, but is still tremendously motivating. It's not just empty management-speak. It's not just a bunch of platitudes bosses deliver in place of cash. In fact, it can be the true reason employees stick with you while you execute change in your company. I know this from experience. When I was on the payroll—before I had a chance to own the company—I know what kept me in my seat and saying no to multiple attractive offers. Lots of other jobs could offer me a paycheck. But could other jobs offer me psychic compensation? I knew that most bosses just don't understand the impact of this approach.

First and foremost, psychic compensation is about autonomy. Everyone wants to be trusted. Everyone wants to be treated like an adult. That's the core benefit here. When you offer autonomy to an employee, you are delivering one of the most valued elements of psychic compensation. Great managers have long advocated autonomy as a motivational strategy. Jack Welch once said that the key to success is finding great talent, giving them ambitious goals, and then getting out of the way. It's the getting out of the way part that really hammers home the benefit to the employee. From that start, an employee will feel trusted and empowered. And any success that follows from that start will be felt both personally and professionally.

How much autonomy can you afford to give? It is an income stream that must be managed carefully. Certainly it must be given throughout the organization; an AOE system demands that workers be willing and able to function without a lot of handholding. That said, you as the CEO will need to be smart about how much autonomy is offered and when. My experience has been that new employees (or young employees) need to be offered this element of compensation on a gradual basis, with more following successful behavior. If you are too quick in granting autonomy, you risk leaving an employee to founder. But when it is delivered on an ongoing basis, employees appreciate it and work hard for more. It is a unique and empowering feeling to know that the boss trusts you and that you have power and responsibility within your organization.

Along with autonomy comes complexity. Jobs should engage you on a daily basis to try harder, use your brain, and push yourself to the next level. If you're not learning in your job, you shouldn't stay. I say that all the time to my employees, and I mean it. The entrepreneurial employee needs challenge and complexity in order to blossom. These are the workers who need new challenges every year. These are the individuals who must be constantly pushed into new areas, achieving things they never thought possible. This is as much compensation as anything that turns up in the paycheck, perhaps even more valuable. Compensation alone will not keep an entrepreneurial employee in his or her seat, however. These are people who want more than money; they want the ongoing challenge of the Next Big Thing.

I saw this happen with Alex, one of my young employees who came to us not for money but for a challenge. Alex was bright and highly valuable to his old employer, earning about $20K over the average base salary for his age and experience. Clearly he was a star. You'd think that kind of money would be enough to keep Alex working for his old boss, but it wasn't. He didn't want to stay put and just rake in the traditional compensation. He wanted a challenge. We were able to lure him away for the chance at greater psychic compensation. We offered him the chance to work directly with a mentor, to master the art of social media for the business, to tackle this new and emerging area for a company that would welcome his effort and his energy. On that basis, he quit his old job and came to work for our firm. Money is motivating, but it isn't everything. For smart, ambitious guys like Alex, the potential for complexity and challenge was even more attractive. I know just how he feels; I made similar choices myself when I turned down offers from bigger firms to stay at the growing, emerging, exciting CJP.

Along with autonomy and complexity, I'll add appreciation. It's remarkable how much we all crave a pat on the back for a job well done. When it comes, we're willing to forgive all kinds of hard work and sacrifice. A 2008 study by the Japanese National Institute for Physiological Sciences found that paying people a compliment appears to activate the same reward center in the brain as paying them cash.[2]

Finally, one of the most important elements of psychic income is how it's delivered. My advice on this front is to deliver it often and with sincerity. A study by Globoforce, a management consulting firm, found the delivery system crucial. "The key is have a program designed to recognize employees 'on the spot' and frequently so that his psychic income accumulates throughout the year," says Derek Irvine, vice president of global strategy for Globoforce.[3]

The use of psychic compensation will become increasingly important to employers as the millennial generation takes its place in the workforce. While workers of previous generations may have been more willing to grind it out for a paycheck and count the days till retirement, millennials are looking for a workplace that makes them feel good. "The Millennial generation likes money, is used to it, but they place a premium on their psychic income," says Molly Epstein, an assistant professor in the practice of management communication at Emory University's Goizueta Business School.[4]

How to Play So People Will Stay

Some management theorists wrap the concept of play at work into the psychic compensation category. And they are related, certainly. But I break it out here to give it emphasis and attention. Play is not just play; it's a steel beam that runs through your overall strategy and helps support your overall goals. The way you deal with issues of fun and nonwork activities in your company is a key element that factors into the morale of your firm and the potential success of your AOE strategy.

There is no question in my mind that an Army of Entrepreneurs that works well together and respects and enjoys one another is one that produces better results. I see it all the time in my own workplace. These are the teams that support one another, feed off each other's energy, and present a united front. (Clients love this; it makes them feel well taken care of.) On the flip side, the team that is constantly fighting, competing for client attention, and trading disrespectful barbs is one that rarely produces top-notch work. How do you produce the good team? One way is to play.

Creating opportunities for team members to get to know and like one another should be part of your business strategy. For some, it is hard to think about the offsite gatherings such as happy hours and social events as part of a business strategy. But I'll argue that it has been an absolute contributor to our bottom-line success. The company that regularly facilitates ways to get to know people personally and professionally will function better. And this is especially key for entry-level folks, as the social part of their work experience can be the difference between staying put and bouncing on to the next job.

How do you make this fun happen?

Office parties and events. At CJP we tend to host an office party or social event every ninety days. I know plenty of other owners and CEOs who think this is excessive, but in times of change and challenge we have found these events to be critical and strategic for business. They provide an opportunity for everyone to socialize and chitchat off deadline, which cuts down on watercooler gossip. They help new folks find social allies and blend more quickly into the organization. These events also help people to bond outside the office and get to know one another in ways that are not possible during the frenzied workday.

Professional development. Having fun while learning is essential. We hold quarterly professional development seminars with the goal of executive education and bonding. Following each professional development session we host a company-sponsored happy hour. Folks look forward to both aspects of our seminars. I often notice that people are energized the week or two following a professional development session.

Beyond the formal "play" events, I try to look for ways employees can have fun at work—while working. As managers, we get the best work out of people who are combining their personal and professional interests, a job that feels like playing. I've seen this work many times. A terrific example of this is the story of my colleague Wilson (who is now an equity owner in the company). Wilson came to CJP with a handful of years in the PR industry. Prior to that he was a part-time actor with credits in soap operas and other professional productions. When Wilson was hired, we put him on a number of high-tech accounts. He worked hard and was a strong performer, but it was clear to me that his passion was entertainment. So when the Internet began to emerge as a force, we saw an opportunity for Wilson to bring his version of fun to work.

Wilson dove right in and became an early adopter of infotainment, and he was an immediate star. Among his efforts was the very first openly branded web TV show. The series called *The Temp Life,* developed for a temporary staffing firm, is a comedy focusing on the most treacherous temporary assignments. It has now won more than five awards and was named among the Brightest Ideas of the Year by *Brandweek* magazine in 2008. That project happened because we were willing to tell Wilson to do more than work hard; we encouraged him to find a way to do what he loved to be successful at work. Everyone wins.

Business travel. Fun isn't just about everyone else in the company. It is also about you. As the leader of the Army, you are setting an example every day. People respond to your every mood and cue. If you are having fun while working hard, people see it and can respond to it. In a real army there is a chief morale officer. That's true in an Army of Entrepreneurs as well, and if you are reading this book, that person will most likely be you. So figure out what makes you happy at your work, and show that passion publicly. For me, this means combining my work with my passion for travel.

When I was a child, my parents, who had traveled and lived all over the world, were in love with the United States. We went across the country and to all the national parks, but I didn't step on a plane until my mid-teens. I yearned to see the world. And I viewed work as a way to do it. Because my company focused primarily on financial services work, I thought it would be easy. I could get to the major money centers in the world through my clients. This was part of my personal and professional vision. But our company, when it was hatched, was strictly domestic and had only three employees. It was this passion for the profession, an entrepreneurial spirit, a yearning to travel and experience international business, that drove me to take CJP international. I struck up a partnership with a London-based firm and began to share clients. Soon I was regularly on planes to Paris, London, and Singapore. And because I genuinely enjoyed traveling with my business colleagues, we would often plan weekend trips to destinations near our meetings, to make sure we wrung out everything we could from the experience. My trips to Paris with colleagues and partners are among my most treasured and fun experiences. I felt as if I was beating the system, making money while also enjoying seeing the world. What could be better?

I do my best to help the rest of my team see business travel like I do. Business travel can be a drudgery, but it can be made less painful. If you have a strong culture, where people respect and like one another, it can be an opportunity to spend more time with a team you enjoy. At our firm, our international business affords us the opportunity to travel around the world. But there is nothing worse than flying halfway around the world to sit in a conference room! That's why we encourage folks to take an extra day, often on the company, to enjoy the destination. It's another way to bring the fun into the everyday effort we expect of our Army.

Whatever you choose to do, the important thing is to make these experiences authentic and "on brand" for your culture. Your play strategy must not be ad hoc. And even more important is consistency. Plan an annual calendar of events and stick to it. These regular moments of interaction and activity will allow you to keep morale high; they will also communicate the commitment of the company to its people and the health of its culture.

And finally, if you're wondering what kind of play would inspire your Army, ask them. One of the key functions of an officer should be to watch and listen for cues that tell you what turns your folks on. In some cases, these passions will be irrelevant to the business; in others they could be the difference between having a new product or division (such as Wilson's Internet TV). True entrepreneurs will be very aggressive in presenting their interests and ideas, but latent entrepreneurs will need a push. They will need their officer to suggest ways they can marry their interests and guide their positions. If the officers are uninterested in the passions of their people, you will miss the opportunity to inspire true happiness and productivity at work.

What to Say So People Will Stay

The final critical element to maintaining momentum is probably the hardest: communication. To keep the momentum going, you must be willing to communicate in ways that inspire your Army. This is an area in which many CEOs falter. They are able to give strong, rousing kickoff speeches. But as the months wear on, the communication wears off and there is little to keep employees enthusiastic about the system. Without communication, all your hard work can fall apart in a matter of months.

Communication is especially important during times of workplace stress. A study by Watson Wyatt found that 48 percent of employers surveyed cited improved communications as one of the three most effective options to reduce employee stress. Communication provides clarity and allows everyone to understand the forces at work inside and outside the firm.[5]

How you communicate is your choice and should be based on your personal style and the size and nature of your firm. Communication can take the form of a memo, a speech, individual meetings, or conversations. Or you may opt to use new technology to communicate. The important thing is that you do it on a regular basis and that you bring a level of sincerity to what you say.

One of my primary communication methods is my weekly blog. Often I find it's the opening paragraph that has the most impact. Here are a few recent ones:

The Purpose of the *J Low Down*

I start the *J Low Down* this week by urging everyone to remember why we launched it in the first place—transparency and communication. I have always said "You can ask us any question outside of someone else's salary." That rule remains true at CJP. Our doors are always open. The *J Low Down* is our attempt to "put out the news" and make sure we are communicating on a regular, weekly basis. I realize that the economy inspires more questions, fears and misunderstandings than in the typical business environment. For that reason, again, I urge you to approach us if you have a burning question versus regarding relying on the potentially inaccurate grapevine.

New York Office Update: There Is a Light at the End of the Tunnel; Four Weeks to Finish. After Work Drinks Planned to Celebrate

We are in the final four weeks of our office transformation in New York and I encourage you all to HANG IN THERE. For those especially seated in the pit, it has been a long tough road of dust, paint fumes and construction noise. I want to make a public apology to those who have endured tough working conditions in the midst of the renovation. This week, Dave, Mark R and I are meeting to develop a timeline which we will publish for all to see to illustrate the plan to finish off the space so you can all see that it WILL be done within weeks. We will also be planning an after-hours office party in the new space (date to be determined by Mark R) which will also be on the schedule. Mark R will handle planning the event and making sure everyone can be there.

Thoughts About the Start of the Year

We are off to the races at CJP into 2010 and the feeling of "opportunity" is in the air. I'm not sure I've had a week with as many quality meetings as last week. Among highlights was our pitch to [Company A], [Company B], lunch with [Company C] head of comms, pitch to [Company D] and pitch to [Company E], and the list goes on. The IR team also submitted their response to a monster RFP last week (fingers crossed).

The CJP team has also rallied to our "plea" to project spot as much as possible to meet our short-term revenue needs. As you'll see below, Gina and the team inked a new [Company F] portfolio company, and [Company G] will receive 3 new proposals from CJP by next week. Keep up the great work guys. We must fight the Q1 business "malaise" climate hard so we can start the year strong.

And on that note please don't miss our first professional development session of the year this week.

Why do I highlight these three momentum builders? There's a theme: It is "let's talk about it." When times are tough, when times are busy, when times are confusing, your staff needs to feel like they can talk to you (or to other managers) about what is going on. This is particularly important in an AOE environment. With so much freedom, staffers may sometimes feel like they are adrift. This is the mood that can eat away at your momentum. Without ongoing communication from you, your troops may lose their sense of direction. Why should they keep pushing forward on this entrepreneurial process if they aren't getting reinforcement from the boss? And the feedback they need can be as simple as hearing from you, on a regular basis, about why the AOE process is worthwhile.

How you communicate, what you say, and how often you say it can be the critical glue that keeps everyone feeling connected and valued. Even when you feel you can't say much, remember to say "good job," "thank you," and "my door is always open." That may do more to keep your AOE process on track than any other effort.

Case Study: Fun at Work

Nobody *needs* a motorcycle.

That's what the president/general manager spent years telling his fifty-plus employees at his West Coast dealership.

"We don't sell transportation, we sell fun," he said. To make that sale happen, he decided, his employees needed to have some fun themselves. Consulting with an outside adviser and using its fun-at-work system, the dealership made changes. Among them:

♦ An offsite meeting at a local bowling alley

♦ Impromptu root beer float parties to celebrate an accomplishment or to recognize someone's particular hard work

♦ Dealership cookouts every Saturday, April through September, for customers and employees

♦ Weekly breakfast outings where managers take their teams out

The results were dramatic. The profits grew, as did the company's customer satisfaction rates. But the other successes were internal. The employee retention rate improved by almost 15 percent. Asked to rate the program, 100 percent of employees thought it was relevant or very relevant to their work. In an employee survey on fun at work, staffers gave their company a 4.15 out of a possible 5.

Most dramatic, says the general manager, was the change in manager mindset that had once held that "work and fun were unrelated." Not only is fun related to work, he found, it's a necessary ingredient to success.

SIX STEPS FORWARD:

What to Do Right After You've Read This Chapter

Momentum is one of the key elements to a successful business that nobody notices until it's missing. Then it's a huge headache to restart. Consider the following first steps to keeping the positive momentum going.

1. Review your compensation strategy. Are you paying for the behaviors that will keep your AOE process on track?

2. Review the compensation plans of your competition. Ask your staff what they've heard about how other companies pay. Can you learn from any of these techniques? Are there processes you can adapt for your own company?

3. Take out your calendar and schedule a series of regular "fun" events. Publicize the schedule so that everyone knows what's in store.

4. Survey the staff: What kinds of activities would they consider fun? Offsite programs? After-work drinks? Silly hat day?

5. Review your communications strategy. How often do you communicate with the staff? Can you boost this frequency? Can you use new methods such as new technology to communicate more regularly?

6. Say thank you. If you've asked your staff to be an Army of Entrepreneurs, you've asked them to step up and work hard. Tell them you appreciate their efforts.

Notes

1. Richard E. Clark, Steven J. Condly, and Harold D. Stolovitch, "Incentives, Motivation and Workplace Performance," Incentive Research Foundation, 2002.

2. Dr. Norihiro Sadato, study for the Japanese National Institute for Physiological Sciences, Okazaki, Japan, 2008.

3. "Employees in Need of a Boost? Give Them a Raise in 'Psychic Income,'" Globoforce, November 2008.
4. "Is Your Firm Ready for the Millennials?" Knowledge@Emory, March 2006.
5. Watson Wyatt, World At Work 2008/2009 Global Strategic Rewards Report.

CHAPTER 11

Managing Disaster

ON A SUNNY DAY, THE WHOLE WORLD LOOKS BEAUTIFUL. WHEN IT rains, only true beauty shines through. This philosophy applies to business strategies too. When everything is going well, it's easy for most managers to look good. When the economy is humming, the staff is happy, and the world around you is relatively stable, whatever you are doing is going to look pretty smart. What evidence is there to the contrary?

That's why you can never tell the true strength of a strategy until it has weathered a disaster. It's during a disaster that the fault lines show. That's when you put your strategy to the test. Does it help you get through the tough times? Or does it act as a drag on your efforts to survive? Sometimes strategies must endure this trial by fire before anyone can be sure if they work or not.

The good news is that the AOE strategy has been battle-tested, even disaster-tested. And it works, even in disaster mode. In this chapter, I'll show you how it has worked for CJP as well as how it has worked for other companies. And I'll explain how the AOE system functions in disaster mode, and how it can even save your business.

How We Have Managed Disaster at CJP

The more we applied the AOE process in our business, the more we were able to see the results. It was never clearer to us that we were on the right path than when we found ourselves in the middle of a crisis. Often that's when it became most obvious that the AOE strategy was enabling all of us to work to our best and highest efforts.

Economic disaster. This is the story of how CJP not only survived the Great Recession, but thrived, thanks to the AOE process. I have mentioned this in passing throughout the book. Now here's the full story.

Like many companies, we enjoyed an upswing during the boom years following the recession of 2001. When the dot-com implosion gave way to some expansion years, we benefited. In 2006, 2007, and 2008, we increased clients, staff, and revenue. We were a firm on the rise.

Of course, that was true for a lot of companies. As they say, a rising tide lifts all boats. In 2009, we faced our greatest economic challenge. Crises struck the housing market, the retail market, and, close to our heart and client base, the financial market. Nationally, growth stalled. Companies began drastic cutbacks in staff and spending. We saw once reliable clients drop their budgets like rocks. It seemed that weekly in our *J Low Down* blog I was announcing that a client had slashed a budget, cancelled a project, or dropped us. Once-solid relationships were suddenly "up for review." The outlook for us, for our industry, and for the economy at large was exceedingly grim.

It's not uncommon for businesses to "hunker down" in situations like this—pull back on efforts to create and expand and just wait out the worst of the economic nightmare. But that is not the AOE way. For one thing, it's not good business. Hunkering down is really just about closing your eyes and hoping for the best. It's not a sure-fire strategy by any means. What's more, hunkering down is an abdication of your responsibility as a leader. Leadership and growth are not just for good times, they are tools for weathering the worst.

And so in the face of our worst market ever as a company, we tapped into the strategy we had been trumpeting for years.

We called for project spotting, which required the staff to step up and look for work where none was being offered. In one week, we convinced one existing client to hire us to update the company website and another to have us produce a corporate video. We did this every week for the long, hard months of 2009. This was not always glamorous work, and it was not work for which any of the staff could collect Commissions for Life, since these were existing clients. But project spotting was the kind of entrepreneurial can-do behavior that helped us keep nervous clients in the fold, keep the revenues coming in, and keep the business momentum moving forward. No one hunkered down. The Army of Entrepreneurs stepped up.

We also communicated constantly. The September 2009 *J Low Down* was a very difficult entry to write.

've been asked by a few people where we stand as a business . . . I've provided some points below that should help:

Our revenue remains at −3% (a good showing in comparison to the industry/our peers, but still not where any of us want to be).

We continue to experience budget cuts and losses. Since the last Low Down, [Company A] and [Company B] cut their budgets (by about −2K per month and −4K per month respectively) and we lost [Company C] and [Company D]. This is to say, we are not out of the woods yet!

The pipeline is very strong for the fall and winter season, so we are hopeful we will continue to bring on new clients and continue to fight the cuts and losses that we expect to continue into 2010.

Our firm is gaining brand visibility (evidenced by a major increase in "over the transom" inquiries to our Web site) which is helpful in every way.

We continue to invest in the company (tech, intern program, digital practice, etc.).

We are making strategic hires within our existing budget (see below) to ensure we have the bench necessary to handle the work we have and are projecting.

And overall, more qualitatively, I am quite proud of what our team has accomplished. We need to stay extremely vigilant but we are feeling good about the momentum!

And we continued to hire. This was one of the toughest things I have had to do as an executive. The bad news was all around us. The economy was floundering and our clients were in crisis, so how could I possibly think about hiring at a time like this? A traditional management method would have suggested a hiring freeze; an AOE method led me to continue to make strategic hires, even during the worst of the crisis.

When I made a hire, I devoted space in the *J Low Down* to this discussion:

A reminder—CJP considers the career of every EXISTING team member before we make a hire, especially at the senior level. Our existing team members and their opportunities and compensation are our first priority.

Our recent hiring is being made possible by cost-cutting initiatives announced over the past six months. In other words, we have not increased our overall payroll to accommodate hires as the firm's revenue remains − 3% below last year at this time. This is just a reminder to all that we remain extremely conservative as the recession is still very much affecting our business.

We are allocating resources where we believe we will be able to acquire clients in late 2009 and 2010. Our financial services PR business, and more specifically our Wall Street 2.0 practice, appears to be an area of opportunity.

If you have any questions regarding this hire or any others please ask!

How effective was this strategy? It saved us. I'm not exaggerating. When I reviewed the wins and losses for the year, it was clear how devastating the effects of the recession had been on our clients. One-third of our business had gone away. But we were not, as you might expect, down one-third for the year. In fact, we were, all things considered, not doing badly at all. We were up 2 percent for the year. Not a great year, to be sure, but not a disaster. We had no office closings. We had no crushing restructurings of our business. Indeed, while our industry saw pay cuts averaging 10 percent, most CJP staffers got raises. When I gave the opening remarks at one of 2010's early training sessions, I reviewed this experience for the staff and asked them to look around the room. Had we not been committed to an AOE process, one-third of us would not have been there.

We had, thanks to the AOE process, stepped up and replaced what was lost, in the year it was lost. As a result, we saved ourselves from the worst of the crash. I was never more proud of our team or of this process. Tested in battle, the Army came through.

Client disaster. Surviving the economic crisis was obviously an important event for us, but it is not the only time during which I could see the AOE process saving our bacon. It has often been the system of teamwork and entrepreneurialism that has helped us to help clients when they are in crisis.

Tom, our senior vice president, likes to tell this story of CJP teamwork working in crisis:

> We have a specialty at CJP in marine transport. One of our biggest tests came when a ship owned by one of our clients was hijacked by Somali pirates. It was our job to take care of external communications and we knew that while this might include traditional constituencies like the media and government, there is another critical constituency out there: the families of the ship's crew.
>
> Families are understandably very vulnerable in situations like this. Their loved ones—husbands, brothers, sons—are being held hostage by pirates. And the Somali pirates are very good at leveraging families in these situations. We realized our client, the company,

needed to be communicating with the families. They needed to know what was happening, day in and day out, and the company needed to make that connection quickly. But it was easier said than done. The entire ship's crew was based in India; all the families were Hindi speakers. Back here in my office in New York, that was a big challenge to me. I was just about to go outside the firm and hire a translator when Jen spoke up:

"Wait a minute. Isn't Gauri a native Hindi speaker?"

Gauri was a member of our professional services team. She was known primarily in the firm for her skills in investor relations. But I knew this was the kind of place where I could tap her to come in on this team, in this crisis, and step up. And she did. For a week and a half she was the bridge that allowed us to help our client—this big, American company—communicate effectively with distraught families in India. It was her skill—and her willingness to step up and do what was necessary even though it was certainly not in her job description—that allowed us to do our best work for the client.

Could that have happened in a bigger or less entrepreneurial firm? Would we have known that someone over in professional services spoke Hindi? Would it have been so seamless to tap someone from another department to come over and help us in a crisis? Because this firm is so nimble and because that ability to step up is so important to us, when there was a crisis, we were ready.

Talent crisis. If you're running a growing firm, you're always worried about how to handle the war for talent. It's a constant battle. Growth is dependent upon having the right people in the right place at the right time. And that is one of the great challenges of management. Getting the right people is so much harder than it looks. It's particularly challenging to a firm like ours, because we look not just at the resume, but at the individual. That can be a long, detailed recruiting process.

But, as is often the case, the AOE system steps up to help the firm in the talent wars.

In 2006 and 2007, my firm boomed at more than 30 percent a year. It was thrilling, it was gratifying, but it was a huge hiring headache. We needed more people, and not just anyone who could warm a seat. We needed people with talent and drive and a willingness and ability to work in an entrepreneurial environment. We had a big talent need and high talent standards.

So we did what most companies do when they face a talent crisis: hired headhunting firms. They made us a lot of promises about their networks and their connections and how we would soon have our pipeline full of great candidates. Well, we got plenty of candidates, but they were not what we needed. The truth is that we needed a different sort of individual. We needed skills that would not necessarily turn up on a resume. A headhunting firm's process could go only so far for us.

So we tapped the Army of Entrepreneurs for help. I reached out to staffers on a regular basis and asked them to identify people they thought would be a good fit here. I asked them to make contact and talk to these individuals about working at our firm, and encouraged them to be hiring ambassadors to us. This was not a simple process. For one, many companies have "no poaching" rules and regulations. We had to be clear with our staffers that we expected them to play fair and be above reproach at all times. At the same time, it required me to be open and honest with the staff about who we wanted to hire and what our hiring plans were—information that managers in other firms might keep close to the vest.

By empowering our staff to recruit for the company, we were able to attract the talent we needed. Our turnover rate remains low; when we make a hire, it sticks. This is because our Army is willing to pre-screen and help us connect with others who will thrive here.

How Other Companies Have Managed Disaster

We are hardly alone in our experiences. There are many companies that have survived disaster thanks to an AOE philosophy. We've gathered a few of the best stories here.

It's fair to ask: Are these really AOE examples? After all, we at CJP have embraced the terminology and the philosophy. If you asked the companies I profile below, would they say they recognize the term "Army of Entrepreneurs"? Maybe not. But I spotlight them here because even though the companies may not have adopted an Army of Entrepreneurs as a management philosophy, they were showing it in action. These are companies that, when faced with a crisis, displayed extraordinary AOE skills. From my perspective, it doesn't really matter if they themselves identify with the AOE brand name. I see it in their efforts. I know they are one of us and their examples are here to inspire.

Natural disaster. As Hurricane Katrina approached on that Sunday in late August 2005, many of the reporters and editors in the *New Orleans Times-Picayune* newsroom thought the storm would miss them. It didn't.

At first, the dozens of staffers who opted not to evacuate holed up in the newspaper building, sleeping in sleeping bags and on air mattresses, continuing their efforts to gather news and get it to their readers via updates on the newspaper's website. They posted continual updates until the building was evacuated. They traveled in delivery trucks to safety in Baton Rouge, where they were able to set up a temporary newsroom in classrooms at Louisiana State University's communications school.

Over the next days, the newspaper staff continued its job of gathering and disseminating news. Teams of reporters traveled back into swamped New Orleans to gather details. For three days, the publication was only electronic. When the paper was able to put out a sixteen-page paper edition, reporters took the copies over to the New Orleans Convention Center and "people grabbed for them as if they were food," said *Times-Picayune* editor Jim Amoss in an address to the American Bar Association's Communications Forum in 2006.[1]

The journalists who worked that week were not impartial observers. They were residents of the city devastated by the hurricane. Many of them were homeless after the storm. But they stepped up to their task and continued to inform the community of New Orleans during its worst disaster. There are no rules as to how to put out a newspaper when your city, your presses, and your homes are underwater. Each staffer had to be willing to step up and do what was necessary to get the job done. Without that mental commitment, it would not have happened.

The *New Orleans Times-Picayune* was awarded the Pulitzer Prize in 2006 for public service and breaking news reporting.

Facing obsolescence. U.K. firm Martin Mulligan was struggling to stay afloat in a competitive marketplace. In 2000, the printer of bar codes was finding it hard to find new customers.

When temporary student employee Adam Hughes arrived for his two-week internship, the problem was immediately clear to him. Martin Mulligan was using outdated marketing methods. To find new customers, it was relying on direct mail and telephone sales. Hughes suggested a change to a web-based marketing program.

Given a green light, Hughes put a web-based ordering system in place, and the company was quickly able to secure in the neighborhood of $1 million in new contracts, including one from the United States worth $100,000, the company told the *Times* newspaper in the U.K.

Martin Mulligan offered its temp whiz a permanent position as head of marketing for its U.S. business. The student declined, opting instead to return to his architecture studies.[2]

Who's the hero of the story? At first blush, it's the young Mr. Hughes. But Martin Mulligan's management deserves credit for the save as well. It takes a manager open to an AOE system to take advice from the temp.

Offshoring. When a manufacturing operation bogs down, some companies call in a consultant. But one company executed a turnaround by turning the process over to its workers, and the consultants simply chronicled the event.

Isola, a manufacturer of electronic materials in Duren, North Rhine–Westphalia, Germany, was a company facing problems with speed and errors. Management was wondering if it would not simply be easier to improve profitability by closing the factory in this high-wage market and offshoring in a new location, cutting labor costs and starting over.

Instead, management turned the problem over to the workers to solve. From the start, it was made clear that improved efficiency was the job of everyone on the staff.

Results were dramatic:

♦ Tons of useless materials were identified, including 100 cubic meters of extra packaging materials and 150 pallets of empty barrels.

♦ More than 800 suggestions for improvement filled the various suggestion boxes. Most of them were eventually implemented.

♦ Manager office space was converted from traditional walled offices to a more open plan. Workers were encouraged to drop by any time with suggestions or comments. Managers even stopped wearing coats and ties, opting for rolled up sleeves, to convey their buy-in to the new can-do attitude.

In addition, the error rate declined and bottlenecks were erased. Instead of calling on outside consultants to give orders, the company engaged its Army of Entrepreneurs to lead it out of inefficiency. A factory facing offshoring was able to stay put.[3]

Learning from Disasters

If there are so many examples of the AOE process as a business-saving device, does that mean it is being more widely adopted?

In some areas, AOE thinking is taking hold. For example, when you look back at the way it helped keep the German manufacturer, Isola, open, you can see that what happened inside those four walls was management's mandate to the staff to stop waiting for orders and start innovating. Innovation is one area that business is increasingly adopting as a necessary strategy.

Innovation is a top priority for companies seeking to grow in the wake of the economic downturn. A collection of studies released by Accenture found almost half (48 percent) of executives surveyed in the United States and the United Kingdom said their companies had increased funding for innovation in the preceding six months, while one-third (33 percent) said their innovation funding remained the same. Additionally, nearly nine out of ten respondents (89 percent) said that innovation is as important as cost reduction to their company's ability to achieve future growth, if not more important. "Companies can't afford to avoid risk; they must learn from their mistakes and make the bold moves required to grow their company and position it for the economic upturn," says Mark Foster, Accenture's group chief executive of global markets and management consulting.[4]

With more firms supporting innovation, more will naturally move toward the operating system that allows creative thinking. Perhaps they are not planning to raise and deploy an Army of Entrepreneurs, but if the mandate from the corner office is "innovate or die," that will require a level of independent and entrepreneurial thinking. Order takers don't come up with great new innovations.

But while innovation may be taking hold, other elements critical to AOE thinking remain untapped by the majority of business leaders. Think back for a moment to the example that is closest to my heart: CJP's experience during the Great Recession. It could not be clearer to me that entrepreneurial thinking, behavior, and operations saved us and positioned us for success going forward. But that's not a concept that has caught on. A study by A. T. Kearney looked at businesses that wound up in bankruptcy and found that in most cases, the economy was not to blame. "The root of insolvencies is often strategy. Managers often react too late and again lack strategic foresight. Enterprises are paralyzed; although the crisis is omnipresent, it is often underestimated and counteractive measures are taken too late," says Robert Ziegler, vice president, A. T. Kearney Middle East.[5]

When businesses fail to embrace a smart long-term strategy, the worst eventually catches up with them. They float along during strong economic times, and when the tide goes out they are stranded. They may think the economy is to blame, but the Kearney study shows that's not the case.

Top reasons for insolvency include incorrect strategy/investment decisions, a cost structure that is too high, insufficient liquidity, and belated or inconsistent response of management. Other reasons include value chain dependency, management conflicts, and conflicts between workforce and management. Sometimes, but less often, insolvency is caused by outside forces such as an economic crisis or an industry crisis.

And yet, even armed with that information, we do not see companies stepping forward with an AOE response. How do companies respond to financial woes? Kearny found the top responses are freeing liquid capital, seeking cooperation from customers or suppliers, cost reduction, and taking debt and equity capital measures. Other strategies include seeking better strategic alignment, staff reduction, and communication enhancement. Some companies go outside for help, seeking outside consultants or support from public subsidies.

The most useful AOE tactics—communication and process improvement—are buried on that list. While businesses are learning that innovation is a critical strategy, many are missing the opportunity to use Army strategies to combat economic woes.

Perhaps most worrisome is a study by Marsh Crisis Consulting. Its research found the following attitudes among CEOs:

♦ 85 percent of CEOs said they expected to face a crisis.

♦ 50 percent said they had a crisis management plan in place.

♦ 97 percent of all CEOs expressed confidence that with or without a crisis management plan they would handle a crisis successfully.[6]

It's the last attitude that will be the undoing of many companies. Those are the cowboy CEOs, the ones who think they can muscle through anything, go it alone, be the lone hero. That may be romantic, but it's not useful in today's marketplace. The companies I've discussed in this chapter survived because they evolved past the notion of a single solitary leader at the helm, taking all the credit and responsibility. They survived because they recognized the value in stepping back from that one-man leadership process and learned to let their people dig in and be part of the success story.

Disaster stories are only as good as their lessons. These lessons are for all businesses. The AOE system doesn't just look good on a sunny day; it works when the clouds roll in. That is, of course, if you've made the commitment to embrace the process before the rain starts.

SIX STEPS FORWARD:

What to Do Right After You've Read This Chapter

1. Review your innovation strategy. Does it use AOE thinking?

2. Review your recruiting strategy. Are AOE principles in use?

3. Review your natural disaster plan. Does it tap into the strengths of an Army of Entrepreneurs?

4. Consider some recent crises in your company. They can be true disasters or simply hiccups encountered along the way. Did you respond using AOE principles? What could you have done differently that might have changed the outcome.

5. What would your role be in a disaster? Consider your own disaster plan as an executive. Are you mentally prepared to tap your team for help, or will you revert to the Lone Ranger CEO mindset?

6. Look for AOE disaster heroes. Do research yourself and ask your staff for suggestions. Promote these examples of an Army of Entrepreneurs in crisis success stories.

Notes

1. Linda Deutsch, "*New Orleans Times-Picayune* Trying to Report," *Editor and Publisher*, January 16, 2006.

2. "Student Saves Firm from Bankruptcy," BBC News Online, December 28, 2000.

3. "How Employees Can Help Turn a Company Around," *Telegraph,* March 20, 2008.

4. "Companies Make Innovation a Priority for Growth in Aftermath of Downturn but Management Shortcomings Hinder Results, Accenture Research Finds," Accenture, November 10, 2009.

5. "Only 16 Percent of Companies Fail Due To Economic Crisis," A. T. Kearney, September 1, 2009.

6. "Directors and Boards, Corporate Governance and Crisis Management," Marsh Crisis Consulting, January 1, 2002.

Part III
Putting It All Together

CHAPTER 12

Addressing the Naysayers

I'M OF THE MIND THAT SAYS GREAT THINGS CAN AND MUST BE done, with the first step being the mental commitment. Thinking big is part of my natural process and I bring it to my work in every way I can.

That said, the naysayers are out there. I've met them. You've no doubt met them too. They may be managers who fear the loss of their power. They may be staffers who fear additional responsibility. They may be investors who simply don't understand how employee empowerment can possibly be profitable. They may be clients who can only envision a world that revolves around them. An Army of Entrepreneurs is, to many schooled in traditional business practices, a very big idea. You will encounter people along the way who will write you off as crazy for even suggesting such a thing.

For that reason, I'm devoting an entire chapter to the naysayers, what they'll say, how they'll say it, and what you'll need to have in place to beat them back.

Typical Doubts, and Why They're Unfounded

In this section, I'll address the most common worries I've seen crop up during the AOE process. Some surface early, when you've just begun to implement the system, and some emerge later. But what joins all these doubts together is that they are not the insurmountable hurdles the naysayers perceive. They are simply doubts to be dealt with and overcome.

Employees will lose their focus on the work. This is the biggest pushback I get when I talk about the Army of Entrepreneurs. As soon as I mention Commission for Life and linking entrepreneurial behaviors to financial rewards, the panic sets in. Somehow managers have been schooled to believe that employees are so money oriented that they will immediately ditch their training, work ethic, and common sense to chase commissions every moment of the day. I can tell you from experience that it just doesn't happen that way.

When you introduce something new, like a Commission for Life system, you present it to the workforce as an opportunity for individuals to increase their income and help the company. Staffers know they aren't getting new jobs; they're getting a new opportunity to make some additional money and do their jobs better. I've not found anyone confused by this, anyone who thinks their entire job is now centered on Commission for Life pursuits. If anything, I see the opposite, a slower-than-I'd-like adoption of the new behavior. No one suddenly stops doing his or her job.

Employees will care only about work they created. This is really an issue of the quality of the people you've hired rather than the management or compensation system you've set up. In everyone's life, there are priorities. We naturally care deeply about projects we have started, projects we nurture, and projects that add to our financial and professional status. But an AOE is not just a collection of individuals; there is still an important connecting force that binds us. When I encourage individuals to act entrepreneurially, I emphasize two things: the benefits it will bring to each of them individually, and the benefits their behavior will bring to the company as a whole. If you want employees to care about the company—not just about their own slice of it—you have to hire that mindset and you have to communicate it to the existing staff. The AOE is about individual action for individual and company success. Communicate the two priorities and you'll guard against anyone thinking they're in it for themselves.

Sales will be the organization's sole focus. Again, you get what you demand. If you push for additional sales without explaining how this push is organic to the functioning of the larger organization, you risk getting that kind of lopsided behavior. It all goes back to being smart and targeted about your motivational strategies. Motivate—compensate—for the behaviors you want. If sales is the *only* way to get rewarded in your organization, then yes, sales will take precedence over other activities. But motivating for additional sales—along with motivating for other behaviors—will get you a spectrum of results.

Entrepreneurs are born, not made. This one actually makes me angry. Why? Because not only is it not true, it springs from laziness. If you are looking at your staff and wondering where their entrepreneurial skills are, you need to walk over to the nearest mirror, take a good long look, and ask yourself whether you have trained your staff for the skills you want them to have or whether you are just sitting there, hoping they'll come up with skills on their own. Nine times out of ten, the real answer to the question is that you have not done the training necessary to get the behavior you desire.

When I was building CJP and at my wit's end because I felt all the burden of the rainmaking was on me, I had an epiphany. The reason my staff didn't seem to "get it" when it came to generating new business was that they had not been trained, motivated, or compensated to do the kind of tasks I needed them to do. I could tell them what I wanted over and over again. But unless I was willing to put in the hours and commitment to teaching them those skills, I might as well have been talking to the wall.

Entrepreneurial skills are learnable skills. I know this to be true because I took a staff of individuals who frustrated me because they didn't "get it" and developed a training program that helped them develop into successful, productive, entrepreneurial workers. If you want to see entrepreneurial skills in your staff, train them. Put in the time and money to teach them what you want them to do for you. The "entrepreneurial skills" fairy is not going to come down one day and sprinkle magic dust on them. If you want skills you're not seeing, you need to re-examine your training efforts.

Research on entrepreneurship shows that the process can be taught. A research team at Yale University explored this topic when they examined the experience of micro-entrepreneurs. When individuals were given entrepreneurial training, in addition to micro-financing, results in business knowledge and revenues improved. The impact was greatest, they found, on those who expressed the least interest in training before the program began. This just goes to show that entrepreneurship isn't always readily apparent in individuals; sometimes it needs to be drawn out through training and development.[1]

To be sure, some individuals are more naturally entrepreneurially inclined than others. Great! Those are going to be your star pupils in the company training sessions. They will be the ones who "get it" early. Tap their enthusiasm and their natural talent. Highlight their early wins. But do not think for a moment that those are the only ones capable of the process. Indeed, they might not even end up being the most skilled entrepreneurs on your team. Think of it as you would a sport. There are natural athletes. But there are also those who flourish under smart coaching. If the coach simply stood around and waited for the natural athletes to emerge, how successful a strategy would that be?

We don't need to reward lead generation; our brand generates all our leads. If true, that's very impressive. But that's not very common, is it? And frankly, it's poor business practice. If you are currently coasting on the business that floats across your transom thanks to your powerful brand image, it must be a nice feeling. But if I were you, I'd be a bit worried about what might happen if that river were to dry up. What will you do when the economy sours? When a new competitor enters the space? When a rival gins up an aggressive new business campaign? Will you truly be comfortable sitting still and letting your brand generate all your leads? If so, you are sacrificing growth. New business fuels growth. It fuels additional revenue, it fuels your reputation in the marketplace, it fuels your ability to recruit and retain star employees. When you reward lead generation, you reward hustle. What business would not be better off with more hustle?

The issue faced when considering lead-generating tactics is the difference between those who use "attract" techniques and those who employ "seek" techniques. A study led by Chris Pullig, associate professor of marketing at Baylor University, examined the results of realtors nationwide. Those realtors who were outperforming their markets were more likely to use "seek" techniques. They were prospecting proactively for customers. The realtors who used more "attract" techniques, such as signage and advertising, were less successful.[2]

Both sets of realtors were making money. But the realtors in "seek" mode outperformed their markets. Which realtor would you rather be?

Junior people shouldn't be involved in new business. This is the platitude of an old-fashioned, outdated, command-and-control, hierarchical corporate culture. In the old days, age mattered. You were expected to "pay your dues," put in your hours, and allow seniority to dictate your moves up the corporate ladder. People who are used to a seniority system—or are hiding behind it to cover for their own lack of innovation—resist the idea of having junior staff members involved in seeking out new business. Inexperienced staffers may make a mistake, they warn. Maybe. But that's not a good reason to keep them out of the process. Any mistakes they may make will be outweighed by the positives they can bring.

In today's marketplace, junior staffers are often more intimately connected to up-and-coming technologies and marketing opportunities and may be best able to steer the firm in new digital directions. They tend to be highly networked as well, coming into your office with hundreds of virtual "friends." They are fertile ground for new business opportunities, and they should be trained, supported, and motivated to generate new business for themselves and for the company. Some of my biggest success stories in our Army have come from the ranks of my most junior staffers.

This is not to say that junior people know everything they need to know to sail out into the new business system and represent the company. I would modify the original statement in this section to read: Junior people shouldn't be involved in new business, unsupervised. They should be mentored carefully for the best possible individual and company results.

There is too much risk associated with decentralized decision making. There is risk associated with decentralized decision making, that's true. But I'll argue there is a greater risk associated with *not* decentralizing decision making. Centralized decision making is actually significantly more dangerous to a company that wants to grow. If all decision making is kept cloistered in the management ranks—or, worse, in your own office—you set natural limits to your company's growth. The company will grow only as fast as you can process the requests that will pour in every day.

You may feel like you are maintaining firm control on the business, but in reality you have created a dangerous bottleneck. If no one can move forward without your approval, no one will take the initiative or exercise their own judgment. This situation builds on itself—staffers fail to try new ideas because they know the long, arduous approval process will make it painful for everyone. The obvious result is a slowing in your company's growth potential.

The benefits of decentralized decision making have been well documented by academic research. Thomas Malone, a professor at MIT Sloan School of Management, looked at the impact in his book

The Future of Work. Decentralization, he says, has three primary benefits. The first is that it encourages motivation and creativity, the second is that it allows many minds to work simultaneously on the
same problem, and the third is that it makes room in the workplace
for individualism.

These results, he says, were initially most beneficial to companies
in the professional services segment. These are the companies for
which creativity and individualism had the greatest positive impact.
But as business has moved to a more knowledge-based economy, the
need for creativity and individualism has spread to other industries.
Today, there are few business categories that can afford to ignore the
demand for innovation and cutting-edge thinking. All companies
must show those traits in the competitive global marketplace. "The
benefits of decentralization are likely to become important in more
and more places," says Malone. "In fact, in principle, almost any business activity could benefit from having highly motivated, creative
people performing it."[3]

It comes down to this: Do you trust your staff? Have you trained
them so that you believe they possess the skills necessary to be successful? If so, you need to get out of the way and let them do the jobs
you trained them for, the jobs you compensate them for. If you don't
trust them, you have to go back to your training and hiring process
and figure out why that is so. Do you think they're not ready for a
decision-making role? Why not? What do they need to be ready for
that role?

Problems You'll Encounter, and How to Solve Them

In any big initiative, there are challenges that crop up along the way.
Some emerge quickly. Others evolve over time. Here are some to
watch for.

Fear. You are most likely to see this early on, when everything you are
saying sounds unbelievably risky and, well, new. People often fear

what is new. As much as the old system of centralized decision making and command and control stymies growth, people are often still afraid to change. At least the old ways are familiar. This new system you're proposing, who knows?

One way to fight fear is through communication. Fear takes hold and spreads when the only people talking are the ones who are frightened. That floods the zone with negative and worrisome talk. You need to be ahead of that wave. Communicate with your staff, with your managers, with your new hires, about the AOE system, about what you as the leader will do to ensure it is successful. Employees worry especially when they think the boss has come up with a great new idea—and it's their job to make it succeed. Be clear that you, too, are 100 percent invested in making this system work for everyone at the firm. While I use my blog to show appreciation to my staff and to share their successes, I also use it to tell everyone what I've been up to in the past week, what I have been doing to support the Army of Entrepreneurs and to help the company grow using AOE principles. This communication keeps the message positive.

Another way to fight fear is through accessibility. If you say your door is always open, mean it. If you are willing to hear from staff members about their concerns, make time so that this exchange of views can happen. Fear sets in when a concern is raised and there is no one in authority to address it. If you are accessible, you have a better chance of hearing that concern and addressing it before it festers.

Finally, another important way to combat fear is to acknowledge that it, like many negative emotions, is a common workplace phenomenon, one that can be addressed by your actions as company leader. A study by Towers Perrin found that roughly 40 percent of employees in a national survey experienced negative emotions about their jobs, everything from lack of faith in management to anxiety over job security. Those who were able to keep their negative emotions in check had some common experiences: They felt a sense of confidence and competence in their work, they felt they had control over their work, and they felt they were part of a workplace community. By providing a workplace where workers are valued and trusted, you take significant steps toward reducing the impact of emotions such as fear.[4]

Inertia. Sometimes an idea is so enormous that people have trouble processing it. The AOE system is not like the workplaces most are used to. When you bring these ideas to your staff, or to new individuals joining your company, you may get the period of "deer in the headlights" syndrome. This may be especially acute for people who were successful at another organization and are now joining your team. The reality of functioning in an AOE environment sets in and the striking difference in demands and everyday behavior become real.

Combating inertia is actually not difficult. It's a question of breaking down the steps and giving the workers time to adopt the behavior in stages. Perhaps not everyone is ready to immediately tackle the terror of a cold call. But that doesn't mean holding off on building and executing those "finding" skills. Be clear about the different ways your staff can execute your strategy. The more points of entry you can offer, the fewer excuses everyone will have to hold still.

Halfhearted effort. What do you do when you sense that some people are just going through the motions? It's a common problem in any company, and particularly in a company going through a culture change such as moving to an AOE strategy. The problem is that the business world is full of strategies. As a result, some employees are cynical about them. To some, your push for an Army of Entrepreneurs is just the Strategy of the Week. They may expect that next month you'll be back with some other brand-new idea for them to embrace.

One sure-fire way to combat cynicism is to put your money where your mouth is. That's why I led off this book with a discussion of Commission for Life. If you want to let everyone know you're serious, follow up your training sessions with news of the first Commission for Life recipient. If anyone thought you were just handing out corporate doublespeak, a check will change their minds.

Along those same lines, look for ways to reward early efforts. If the Commission for Life bar hasn't yet been cleared, what else can be celebrated? Can you spotlight the efforts being made? It can help stragglers pick up their own pace and be more involved.

Loss of momentum. Perhaps everything got off to a great start but now you're months into the new system and things seem to be slowing down. What can you do? I discuss this in detail in Chapter 10, but I'll briefly outline here some ways to jump-start momentum:

♦ Distribute training efforts over the year. If you bunch them all together, you risk losing the impact. Have them scheduled on a regular basis—once a quarter, once a month, whatever interval works for your company. But to maintain the momentum, don't let too much time elapse between sessions.

♦ Schedule fun. Look for ways to connect fun with the AOE program. Schedule training sessions offsite and follow them up with a party.

♦ Remember your officers. I focus a lot on training staffers to execute the AOE strategy, but it's just as important to keep your managers engaged and enthused. If momentum is flagging, it may be because they are lapsing into old management habits. Connect with managers on a regular basis to be sure they understand their role in keeping the forward motion of the Army of Entrepreneurs in gear.

Rookie Mistakes, and How to Avoid Them

As I've engaged the Army of Entrepreneurs in my company and coached others as they pursue it in their own businesses, I've come to notice some common early pitfalls in the process.

Lopsided training. In the early months, it's tempting to lean heavily on the most exciting new parts of the program. It's not uncommon, as a result, to have some difficulties getting the right balance.

I look at it this way: If I want a team of Finders, Minders, Binders, and Grinders, then I have to be training and compensating for those behaviors concurrently. They all need weight and time and support from me. If staffers begin to feel that I favor one over the other three, they may tilt their efforts in that direction. That's a natural tendency, and it's certainly accentuated if you add a financial bonus such as Commission for Life. To avoid this kind of lopsided behavior consider these questions:

- Does your training provide balanced advice? Are you teaching all the concepts you want to see in equal weight? Are you avoiding the appearance of favoring one (such as new business) over another (such as existing client management)?

- Are you surveying your employees after training sessions? That can help you to understand how you're being perceived. After training, ask them to tell you what they've learned, how they think this will impact their day-to-day jobs, what changes they plan to implement as a result of the new training. This feedback will guide you in balancing your training and your instructions, and it will warn you if you've become too lopsided in your information.

Forgetting to celebrate. Creating and maintaining an Army of Entrepreneurs is a journey. There is no finish line, no point at which you can declare victory. It is a way of running and growing a business. As such, it's easy to simply start it and forget to celebrate the gains along the way.

This celebration process is especially important in the beginning. You're asking people to do something different. You're asking them to behave in new ways, add new skills, and think of themselves in new roles. The early gains may be small ones, but they should be celebrated with feeling. I often use my weekly blog to highlight successes. They may not be the big wins—the signed client, the won prize—but they can be small ones. Perhaps someone successfully scheduled a meeting or made a connection with a network of potential new business. Those are AOE gains and as the leader, you want to recognize them and let your staff know you appreciate them.

Sometimes, it won't be appropriate to make a big public celebration of a gain. There are many times when we are training an individual—perhaps someone new to the company or new to a management role—when publicly noting the small, early steps is critical to setting up the bigger wins later on. I recall when we began training one new management employee, we intentionally set her on tasks that might have been considered "low-hanging fruit" to an experienced Army member. But to the new manager, they were a challenge. And when she was successful, I made sure she knew that I'd noticed and appreciated her efforts.

Also, just as training can become lopsided, celebration can suffer from that same imbalance. If you're celebrating one category in the Finder, Minder, Binder, Grinder group, be sure to give the other categories their due applause. When you want all four behaviors, you need to communicate that by celebrating all four behaviors. Winning a big new client can be a lot more exciting than continuing to service an existing client. But if both are important to you (and they should be), then both must get recognition on a regular basis.

Case Study: They Said It Couldn't Be Done: The IBM Turnaround

To call IBM a giant is an understatement. It looms large both in physical size and in impact on the global business world. So what is it doing as an example of AOE thinking? It is a classic example of how good can come to a company when a leader brushes off the naysayers and taps the Army to do its best work.

In 1990, IBM was the second most profitable company in the world. But it was in trouble. As the market for its mainframes was drying up, the engine that had fueled the company's growth was stalling out. Starting in 1991, the company began losing money, bleeding nearly $16 billion over three years.

Lou Gerstner, who joined IBM as CEO in 1993, turned the company around. And he did it in part by embracing a radical idea: empowering his Army to make decisions.

Gerstner did not take the most ambitious decentralization route, the breakup of IBM into a collection of independent units. But he did look for ways to decentralize the decision-making process that was impeding the company's growth process. While critics said this would result in chaos within the company, Gerstner opted to tap the talents of his workforce.

Among his efforts: He restored the line manager's accountability and ownership. He charged his senior managers with redesigns and gave them the power to make sizable changes. The charge to the senior managers signaled the change throughout the company. It would no longer be the case that decisions would be held up in committees at the company's Armonk headquarters. Line managers were to make decisions, and they would be held accountable for them.

This was just one of the many changes Gerstner instituted at IBM, but it was also one of the most lasting and impactful. By 1994, IBM was back in the black. While the job was not finished, the turnaround was clearly in progress. The naysayers were wrong. Empowering individuals to make decisions—even in a company as large as IBM—can have dramatic positive results.[5]

SIX STEPS FORWARD:

What to Do Right After You've Read This Chapter

Naysayers aren't fun, but they are a fact of life in the business world. Here are some steps you can take to stay ahead of the problem.

1. Survey your managers. What doubts are they harboring? Help them understand why they're unfounded.

2. Survey your staff. What doubts are they harboring? Help them understand why they're groundless.

3. Survey your clients. Do they know about your AOE process? Are they at all worried? Address their concerns with what you already know works.

4. Review your training calendar. Is it bunched up into one quarter? Does it lean too heavily on sales at the expense of other necessary skills? Look for ways to head off any lopsidedness.

5. Create a celebration calendar. Don't wait for inspiration; set out time in your week or your month or your quarter to recognize whatever good things have happened.

6. Look around for success stories. One way to push off the naysayers is to show them who's already succeeded.

Notes

1. Dean Karlan and Martin Valdiva, "Teaching Entrepreneurship: Impact of Business Training on Microfinance Clients and Institutions," Center for Global Development, January 2007.

2. Chris Pullig, Laura Indergard, Suzanne Blake, and Jacqueline Simpson, "Lead Generation: What Really Works?" *Baylor Business* 2008, http://www.baylor.edu/business/kellercenter/index.php?id = 55741.

3. Thomas W. Malone, "Making the Decision to Decentralize," *HBS Working Knowledge*, March 29, 2004.

4. "Emotional Attachment in the Workplace—Keeping Negative Emotions in Check," The 2003 Towers Perrin Talent Report.

5. "IBM Corporation Turnaround," Harvard Business School Case Study, 2000.

Ten Questions to Ponder

ARE YOU READY TO AMASS YOUR OWN ARMY OF ENTREPRENEURS? Ask yourself the following ten questions.

1. Have you read up on recent trends? It's helpful to immerse yourself in current management theory. It will give you a foundation for your efforts and confidence that you are doing the right thing.

2. Do you have support for your cause? Surround yourself with a team that believes in the model and wants to help you make it succeed.

3. Are you being true to yourself? If you don't believe it, if you cannot visualize it, and if you can't commit to it, you should not do it.

4. Can you keep it simple? We talked about a lot of detail in this book, but the reality is that you need to make it simple. Four workshops a year and two offsites, plus in-depth com-

munication from me once a week—that's basically our program. You need to make your program simple and easy to understand and your message repetitive but simple.

5. Can you bring action, not just words? Culture is created from consistent, repetitious actions.

6. Can you set up some quick wins? Momentum fuels innovation. Set a few folks up for a success, then shout that success from the rooftops!

7. Are you ready to give up control? More decisions will be made without you. Great ideas will come from other sources, and business will come from more directions. This is what you always dreamed of, right? Get ready to grapple with becoming less relevant, less important, and less central.

8. Can you tune out the noise? As Jason Fried says in his book *Rework* (Crown Business, 2010), ignore the real world. You need to tune out the pessimists, the naysayers, and those who want to drag you down.

9. Are you being realistic? The AOE system works. I can promise you this based on my personal experience. But I can also tell you that running a business is full of disappointments and unexpected twists and turns.

10. Have you armed your employees? If you were an employee of your company could you tell me the purpose of the company or the problem it's trying to solve? Could you tell me if you're adding value and how? Could you recount a specific situation where you were able to make a contribution? And can you tell me why you think it's worthwhile to work where you do? Give your people the answers to these questions so they can march forward with you, with confidence.

Yes? Alright, then. What are you waiting for?

Additional Resources

NEVER STOP LEARNING.

No matter where you are on your quest to build an Army of Entrepreneurs, you have never learned everything you need to know to be successful. Every day, innovative leaders are trying new solutions and new processes in their companies. As you move into your efforts to create your own Army, consider yourself a lifelong learner in the space.

Where can you go to learn more about creating entrepreneurial processes in your own business? There are many books, magazines, events, and institutions of higher learning where the latest techniques are being discussed.

Additional Reading

Blanchard, Ken. *Gung Ho! Turn On the People in Any Organization.* William Morrow, October 8, 1997.

Bolman, Lee G., and Terrence E. Deal. *Reframing Organizations: Artistry, Choice and Leadership,* 4th ed. Jossey-Bass Business & Management Series. Jossey-Bass, August 18, 2008.

Collins, Jim. *Good to Great: Why Some Companies Make the Leap . . . and Others Don't.* HarperBusiness, 2001.

Gladwell, Malcolm. *Outliers: The Story of Success.* 1st ed. Little, Brown and Company, November 18, 2008.

Kotter, John P. *Leading Change,* 1st ed. Harvard Business Press, 1996.

Lundin, Stephen C. *Fish! A Remarkable Way to Boost Morale and Improve Results,* 1st ed. Hyperion, March 8, 2000.

Miller, John G. *QBQ! The Question Behind the Question: Practicing Personal Accountability at Work and in Life,* 1st ed. Putnam Publishing Group, September 9, 2004.

Murphy, Mark. *Hundred Percenters: Challenge Your Employees to Give It Their All, and They'll Give You Even More,* 1st ed. McGraw-Hill, October 19, 2009.

Pink, Daniel H. *Drive: The Surprising Truth About What Motivates Us,* 1st ed. Riverhead, December 29, 2009.

Thaler, Richard H., and Cass R. Sunstein. *Nudge: Improving Decisions About Health, Wealth, and Happiness.* Yale University Press, 2008.

Vaynerchuk, Gary. *Crush It!: Why NOW Is the Time to Cash In on Your Passion.* HarperStudio, October 13, 2009.

Welch, Jack. *Winning.* Harper Business, 2005.

Publications

Inc. magazine. Written exclusively for people who run small and midsize businesses and full of practical hands-on information to help you succeed in business. http://www.inc.com

Entrepreneur magazine. http://www.entrepreneur.com/

Family Business magazine. Advice for family business owners and advisers. http://www.familybusinessmagazine.com

Events

GW Summit on Entrepreneurship
www.alumni.gwu.edu/programs/special/entrepreneurship/

Annual Gateway Entrepreneurship Research Conference
www.slu.edu/Documents/business/eweb/GatewayConference 2010.pdf

Futurallia Kansas City
www.marc.org/international/futurallia.htm

Atlanta Competitive Advantage Conference
www.cba.gsu.edu/acac/index.html

Global YES Summit—"Rework the World"
www.reworktheworld.org

European Conference on Innovation and Entrepreneurship
http://academic-conferences.org/ecie/ecie2010/ecie10-call-papers.htm

Education

The following MBA programs are well regarded for their teaching and supporting of entrepreneurship:

Babson College "Entrepreneurship is more than just an academic discipline at Babson—it's a way of life. Connecting theory with practice, we infuse entrepreneurial thought and action throughout our curricula and co-curricular activities." http://www3.babson.edu/eship/

University of California–Berkeley "The Lester Center for Entrepreneurship and Innovation is an internationally recognized program and the primary locus at Berkeley for the study and promotion of entrepreneurship and new enterprise development." http://entrepreneurship.berkeley.edu/main/about.html

Massachusetts Institute of Technology "The MIT Entrepreneurship Center team provides content, context, and contacts that enable entrepreneurs to design and launch successful new ventures based on innovative technologies." http://entrepreneurship.mit.edu/who_we_are.php

University of Pennsylvania The Wharton School was the first to develop a fully integrated curriculum of entrepreneurial studies. Today, the Goergen Entrepreneurial Management Program, named in honor of Wharton alum Robert Goergen, is described by Wharton as "one of the largest entrepreneurial teaching programs available, offering more than 20 courses to some 2,000 students and entrepreneurs. The faculty of over 20 professors and practitioners teach courses for undergraduate and graduate students and guide initiatives for entrepreneurs." http://wep.wharton.upenn.edu/aboutwep.html

Stanford University The Center for Entrepreneurial Studies at Stanford offers a program focused on case development, research, curriculum development, and student programs. Emphasis is placed on the study of entrepreneurship and venture capital. The Center supports both alumni and students engaged in entrepreneurial activities and describes its mission as: "Promote research on entrepreneurial companies and on topics relevant to entrepreneurs. Graduate students who understand entrepreneurship and entrepreneurial companies. Provide resources for students and alumni embarking on entrepreneurial ventures. Establish relationships with the local entrepreneurial community." http://www.gsb.stanford.edu/ces/

Columbia University The Eugene Lang Entrepreneurship Center at Columbia Business School describes its program as "one of the most comprehensive and respected entrepreneurship programs in the world. The program is more than just a tutorial on how to launch new ventures. Instead, it is structured to emphasize two key components of entrepreneurship MBA students may concentrate on." http://www4.gsb.columbia.edu/entrepreneurship/program

University of California–Los Angeles The Harold Price Center for Entrepreneurial Studies is part of the John E. Anderson Graduate School of Management at UCLA. The Price Center creates a focus on campus for entrepreneurial education and research and it provides teaching, research, extracurricular, and community activities related to entrepreneurship. Working closely with its Board of Advisors, the Price Center describes its goal as "to provide a set of academic and extracurricular experiences that advance both the theory and practice of entrepreneurship." http://www.anderson.ucla.edu/x5840.xml

Dartmouth College "The Tuck Center for Private Equity and Entrepreneurship aims to advance the understanding of private equity investing—the engine behind the entrepreneurial activity that drives global innovation and productivity. The center focuses on macro and micro issues relating to private equity: capital markets, financing structures, governance and entrepreneurship." http://mba.tuck.dartmouth.edu/pecenter/about/index.html

Harvard University The Arthur Rock Center for Entrepreneurship seeks to infuse the overall mission of the graduate program with an entrepreneurial point of view. Founded in 2003 from a donation by venture capitalist Arthur Rock (MBA 51), the Center offers a range of programs and services, including support for faculty research, fellowships for MBA and doctoral students, the annual business plan contest, and conferences. http://www.hbs.edu/entrepreneurship/

Cornell University The university's program, Entrepreneurship @ Cornell, is designed to work across Cornell's schools, colleges, and organizations to help promote entrepreneurship education, events, commercialization, and experiential learning opportunities. "Our vision is to support a diverse group of university-wide activities that finds and fosters the entrepreneurial spirit in every Cornell participant—in every college, every field, and every stage of life." http://entrepreneurship.cornell.edu/

Thinking from Top Consulting Firms

From Accenture: Study, "Liberating the Entrepreneurial Spirit," July 2001. http://newsroom.accenture.com/article_display.cfm? article_id = 3761

From Boston Consulting Group: Article, "Supporting High-Impact Entrepreneurship." http://www.bcg.com/about_bcg/social_ impact/Community_Economic_Developm ent/ImpactStory Detail.aspx?id = tcm:12-24766&practiceArea = Community + % 26 + Economic + Development

From Booz Allen Hamilton: Speech, "Entrepreneurship: It's Not About the Product . . . It's About the Passion," by Dr. Ralph Shrader (Booz Allen chairman & chief executive officer) to the Strategic Management Society Conference, 2000.

Index

About the Author

Jennifer Prosek is the founder and CEO of CJP Communications where she leads many of the firm's key accounts. Under her leadership, the firm has become a leading international public relations and financial communications consultancy with offices in New York, Connecticut, and London. With more than seventy-five professionals, the firm ranks among the top thirty-five independent public relations firms in the United States and among the top five financial communications consultancies in the UK.

Prosek has earned numerous honors. She was a finalist for the Ernst & Young Entrepreneur of the Year award in 2010 and was named an "Emerging Power Player" by *PR Week* magazine in 2009. She was also inducted into the Arthur Page Society, which includes chief communications officers of Fortune 500 companies and CEOs of the world's leading public relations agencies. CJP was named "Small Agency of the Year" by *The Holmes Report* in 2008 and a "Best Agency to Work For" in 2008 and 2009.

Prosek received her MBA from Columbia University and her undergraduate degree from Miami University in Ohio. She is a frequent speaker at leading business schools and for entrepreneurial and business organizations. She serves on the board of directors of the New York City Partnership for the Homeless.